Bird Skeletons Copyright-free Images for Artists & Designers

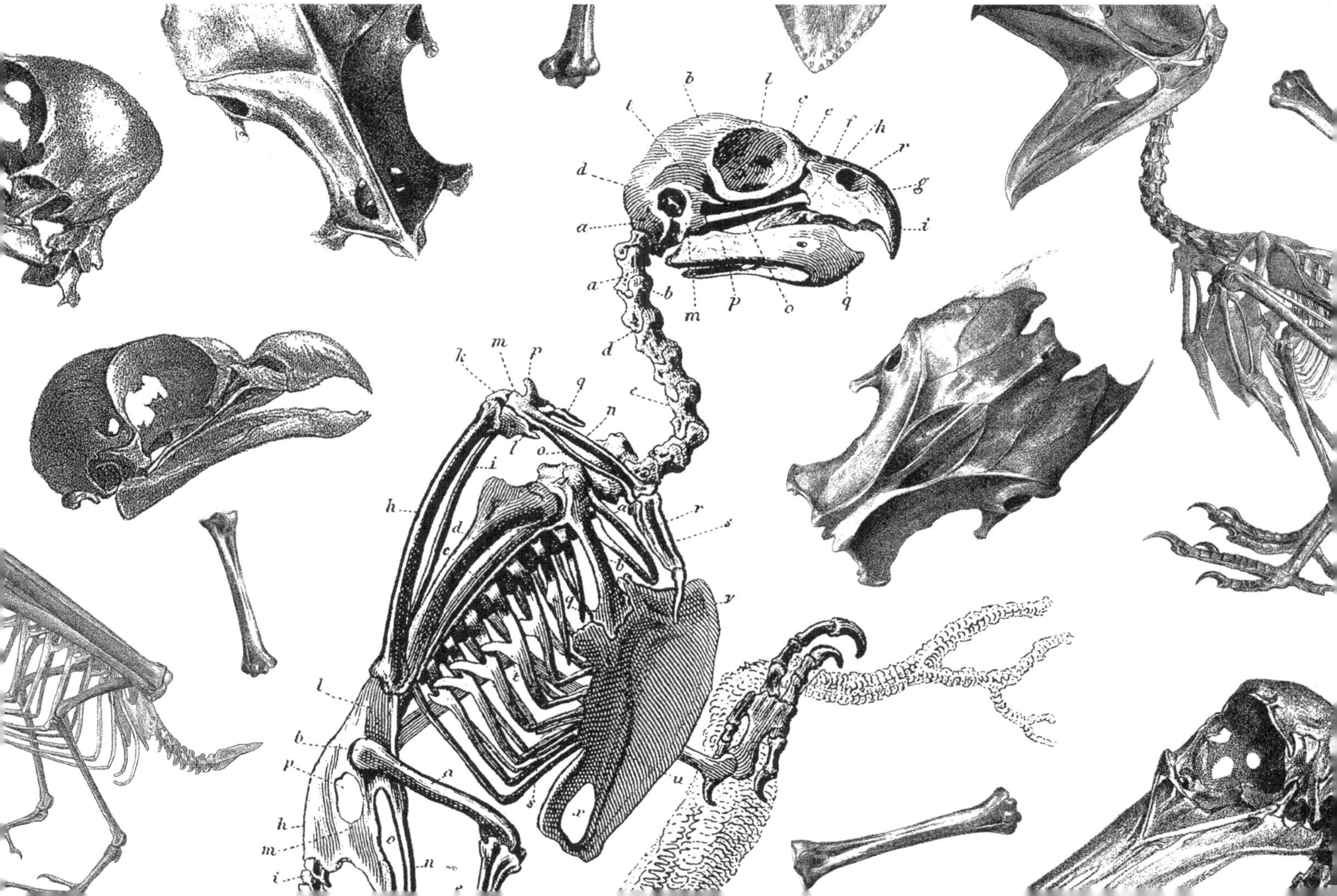

Download Your Files.

BIRD SKELETONS

This 2019 offering from Vault Editions is a brilliantly curated resource of copyright-free vintage avian anatomical illustrations. This book features rare and inspiring artwork from the titles of acclaimed 17th-century naturalists such as Thomas Campbell Eyton and T.Milton. This pictorial archive features a diverse range of over 100 anatomical engravings and etchings from savage birds of prey to flamingos, ducks, swans, cranes, hens, doves, ostriches and much more.

This book comes with a unique download link providing instant access to all images featured. These images can be used in art and design projects, or printed and framed to make stunning decorative artworks.

Download your files via the following link:
www.vaulteditions.com/bird
password: bsvlte2f43s

Technical Assistance:
For all technical queries, please contact
info@vaulteditions.com

Bibliographical note
This book is a new work created by Avenue House Press Pty Ltd.

Copyright © Avenue House Press Pty Ltd 2019.

ISBN: 978-1-925968-06-4

LEARN MORE /
VAULTEDITIONS.COM

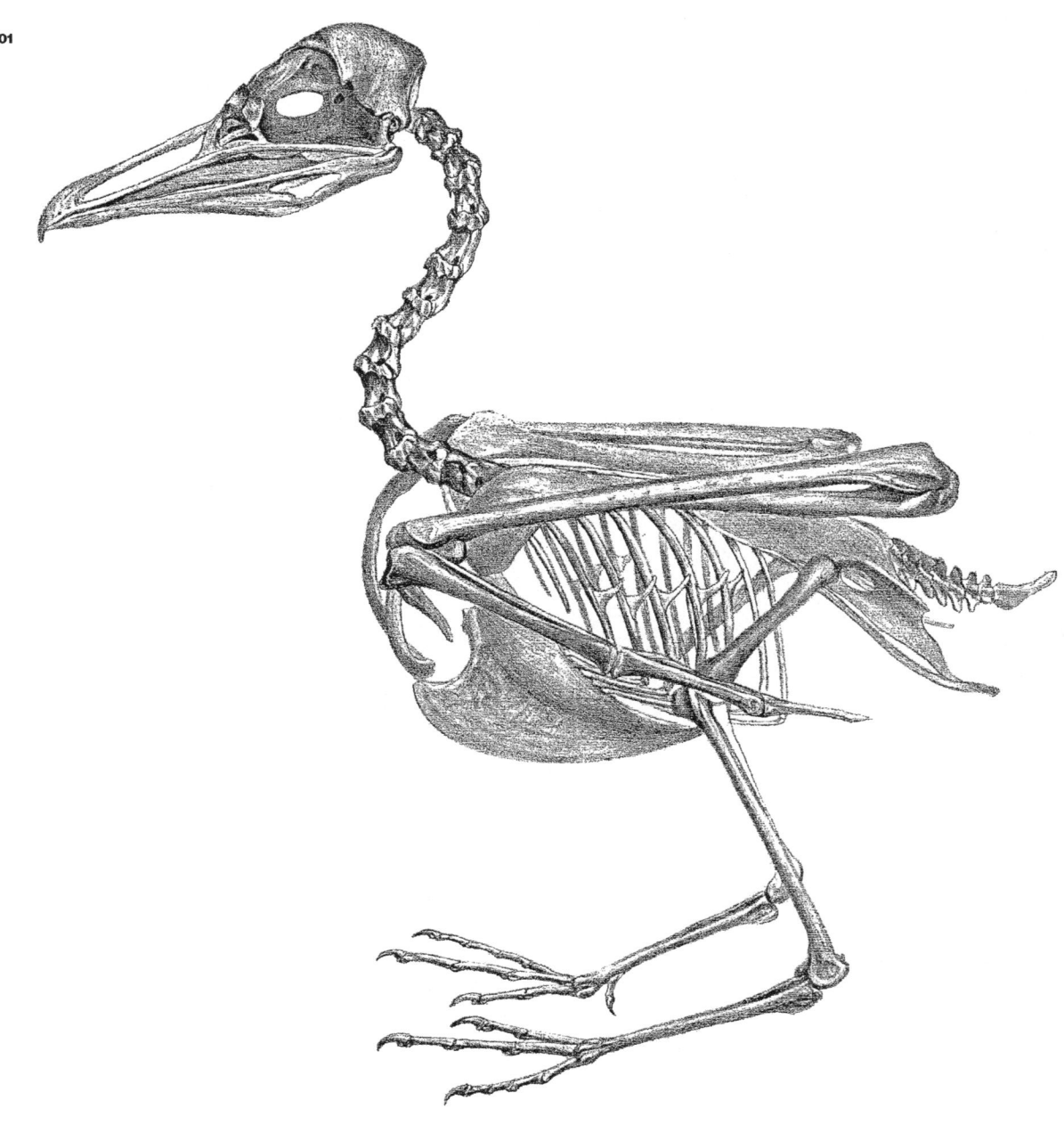

Fig.01 Stercorarius Pomarinus.

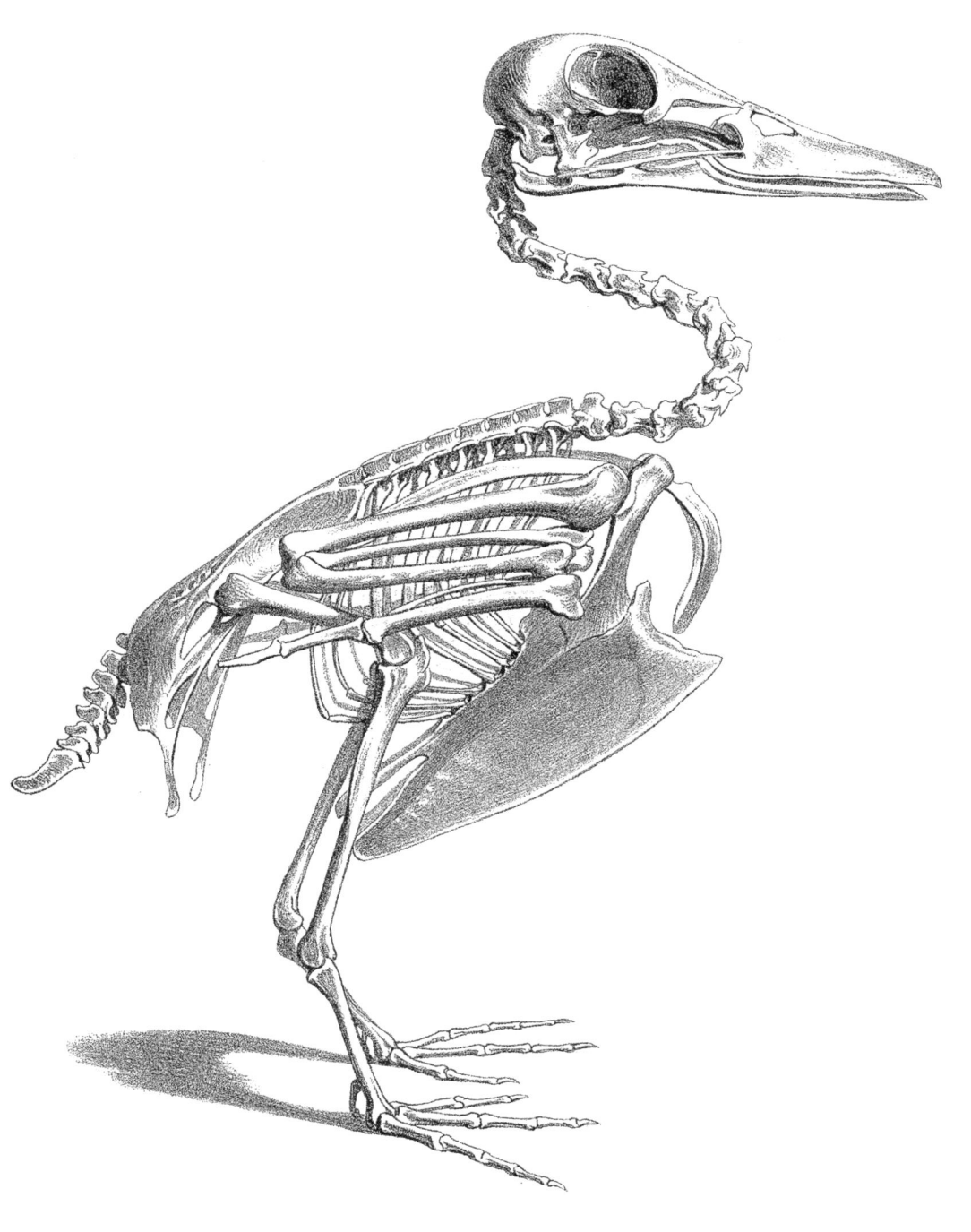

Fig.02 Querquedula Crecca.

Fig.03 Cereopsis Novae Hollandiae.

Fig.04 Anser Cygnoides.

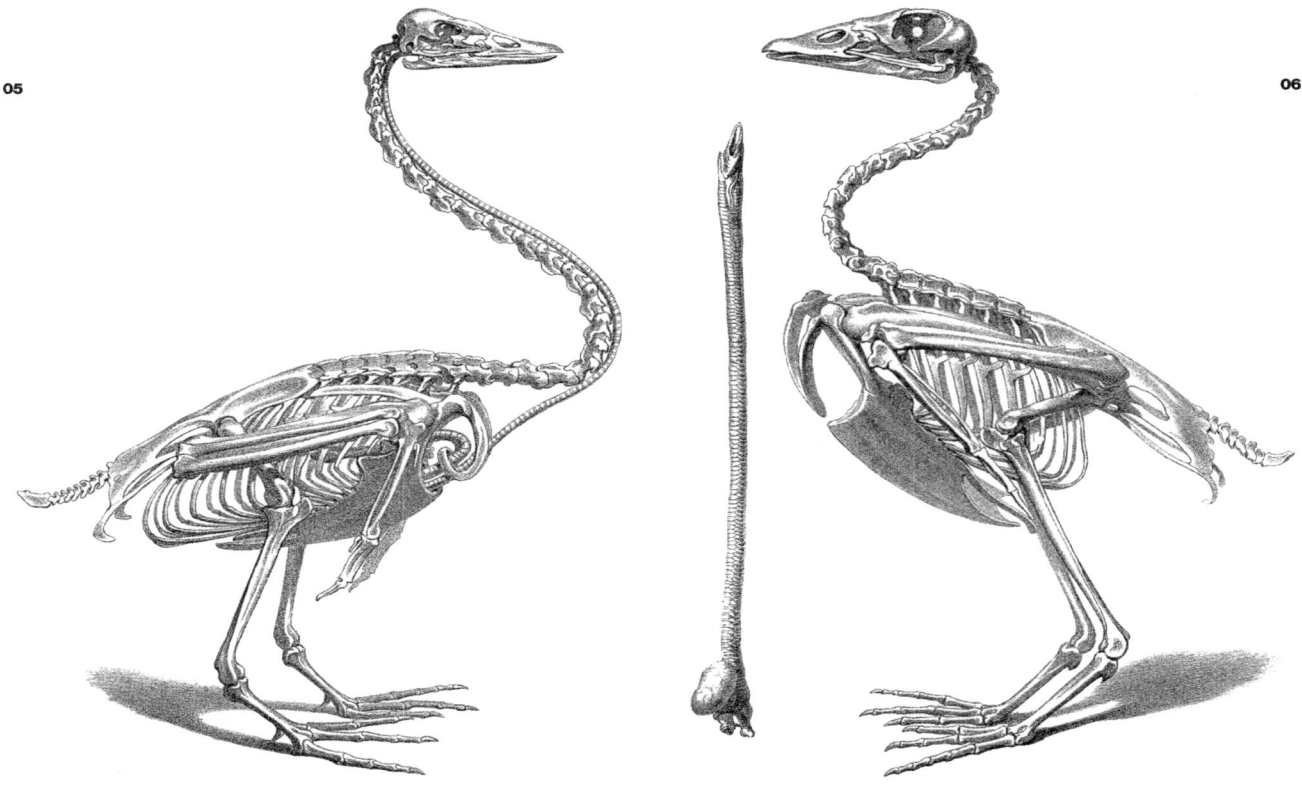

Fig.05 Cygnus Ferus.

Fig.06 Chenalopese Ægytiaca & Trachea.

Fig.07 Tadorna Bellonii.

Fig.08 Dendrocygna Areuata.

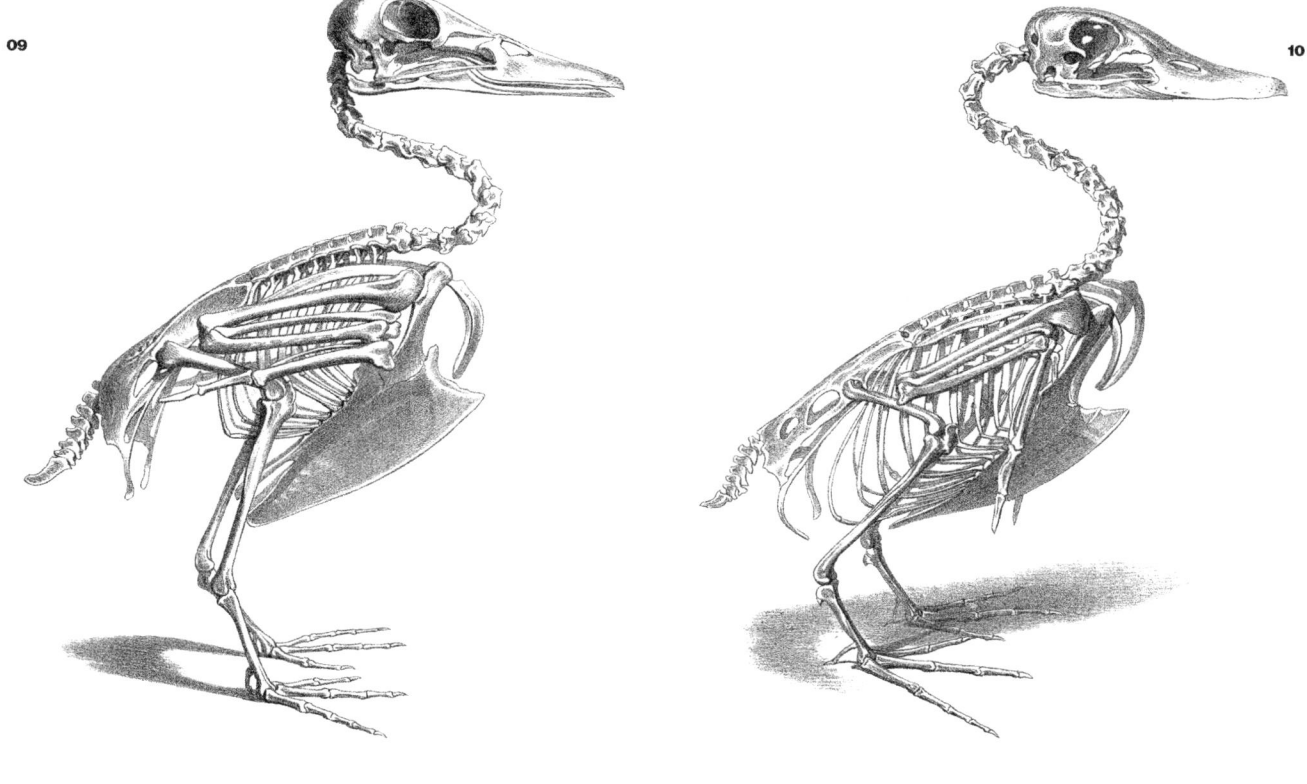
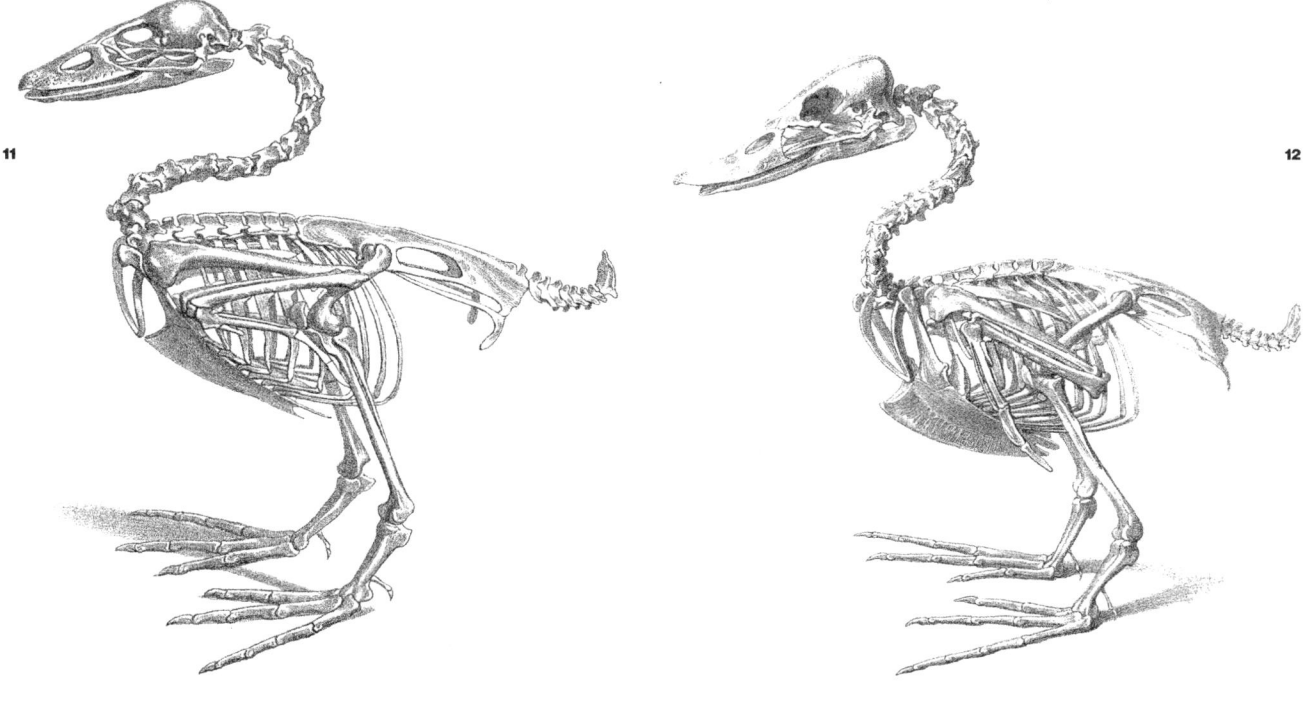

Fig.09 Querquedula Crecca.

Fig.10 Nyroca Leucopthalmus.

Fig.11 Hydrobates Lobatus.

Fig.12 Oxyura (Erismatura) Australis.

Fig.13 Opisthocomus
Christatus.

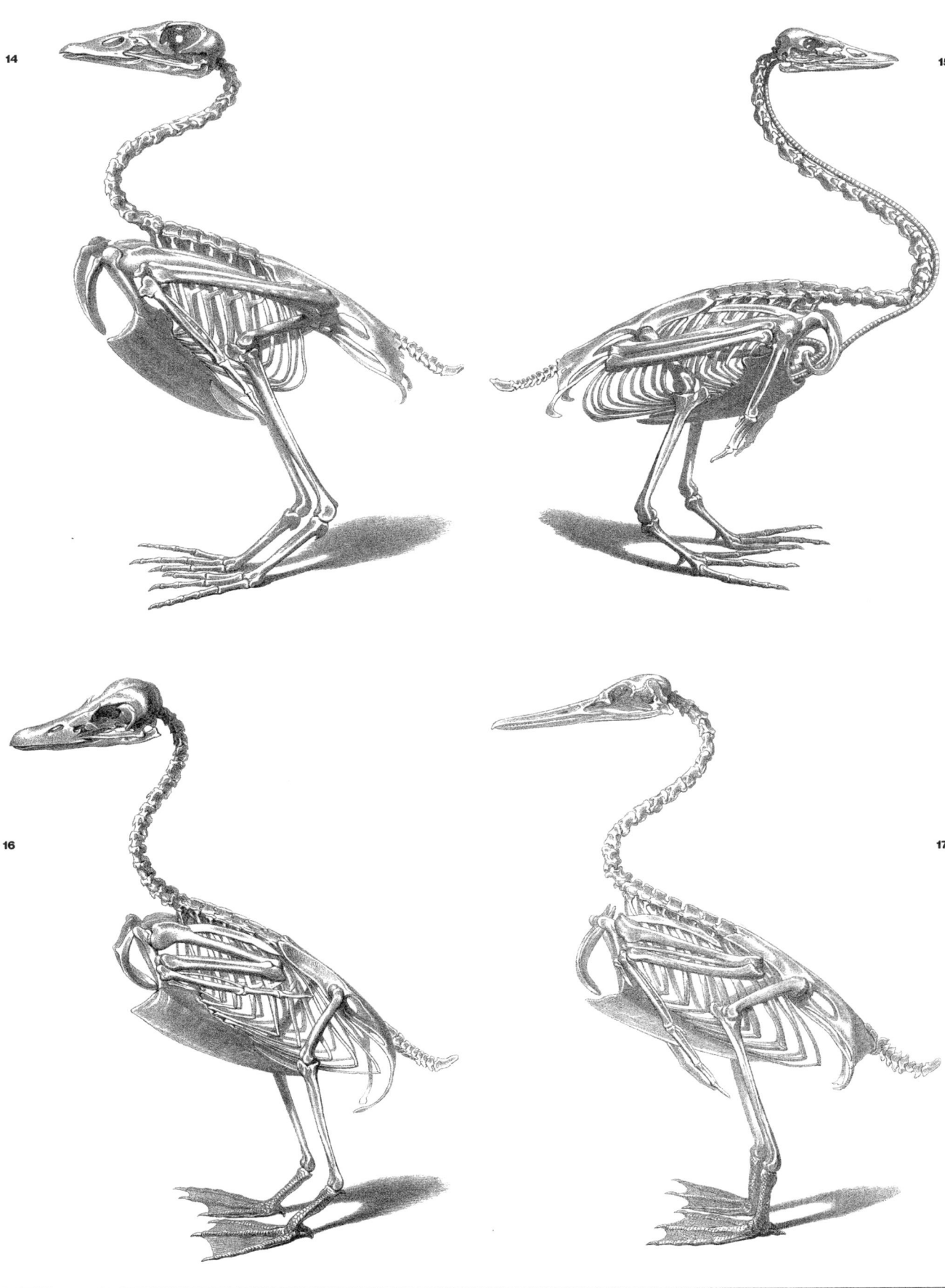

Fig.14 Chenalopese Ægyptiaca.

Fig.15 Cygnus Ferus.

Fig.16 Harelda Glacialis.

Fig.17 Serrator.

Fig.18 Rhynochetus Jubatus.

Fig.19 Centropus Rufipenis.

Fig.20 Zanclostomus Sumatranus.

Fig.21 Struthidea Cinerea.

Fig.22 Ptilonorhynchus Smithii.

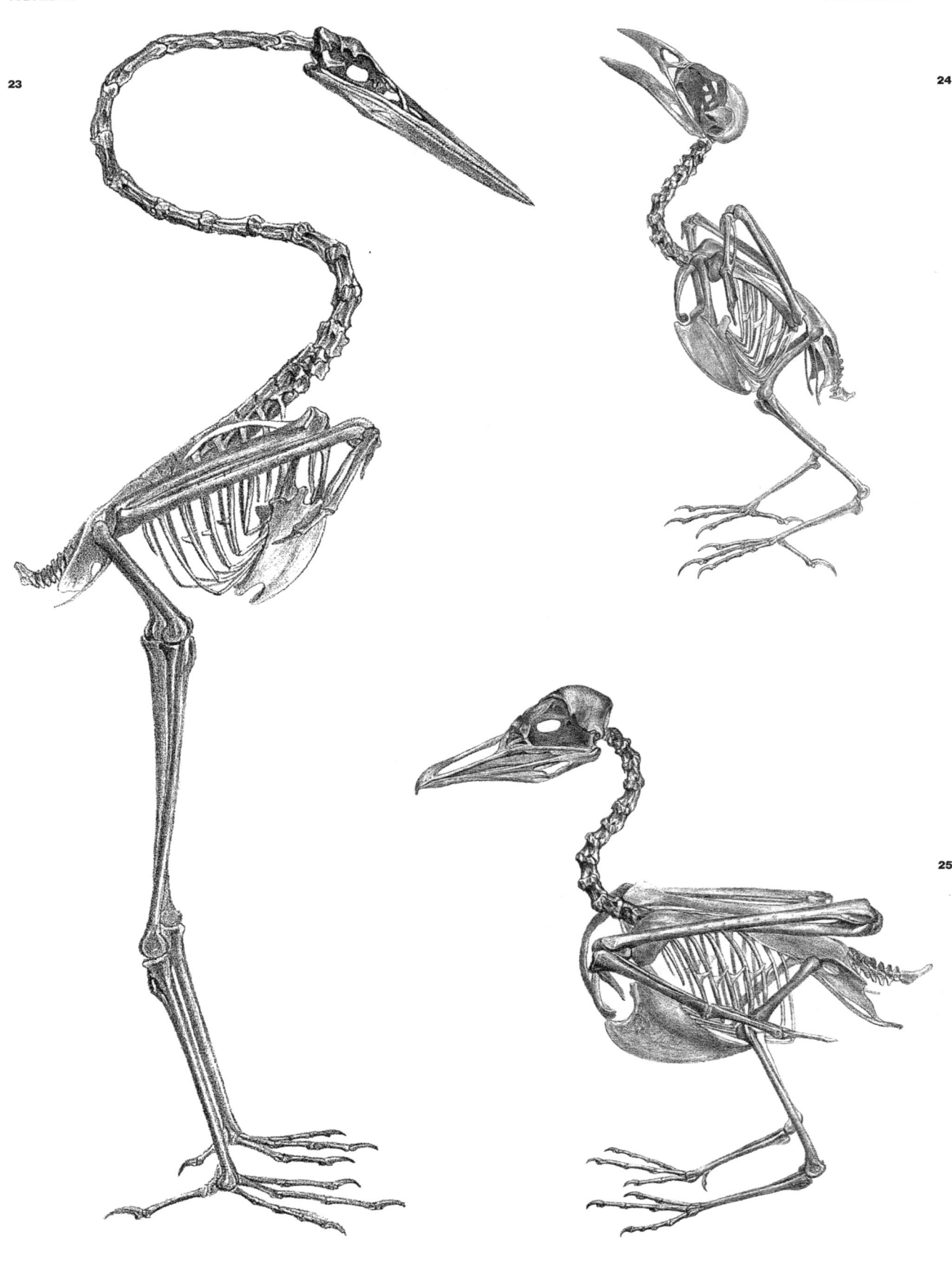

Fig.23 Ardea Herodias.

Fig.24 Dendrocitta Vagabunda.

Fig.25 Stercorarius Pomarinus.

Fig.26 Momotus Cequinoctialis.
Fig.27 Rynchotus Perdicarius.
Fig.28 Crypturus Megapodius.
Fig.29 Ceriornis Temminckii.

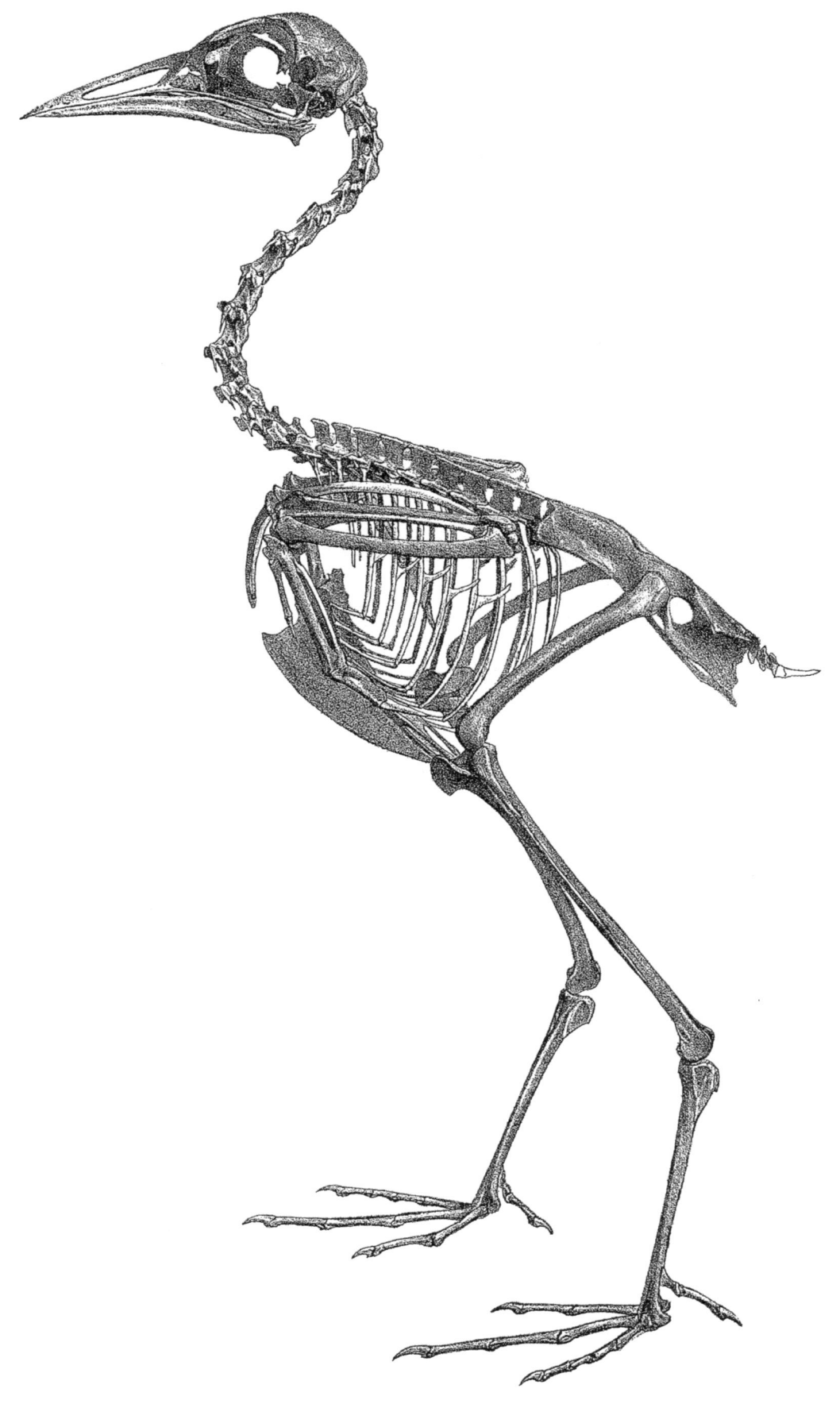

Fig.30 Aramides Cayanea.

Fig.31 Ocydromus Sylvestris.

Fig.32 Antigone Torquata.

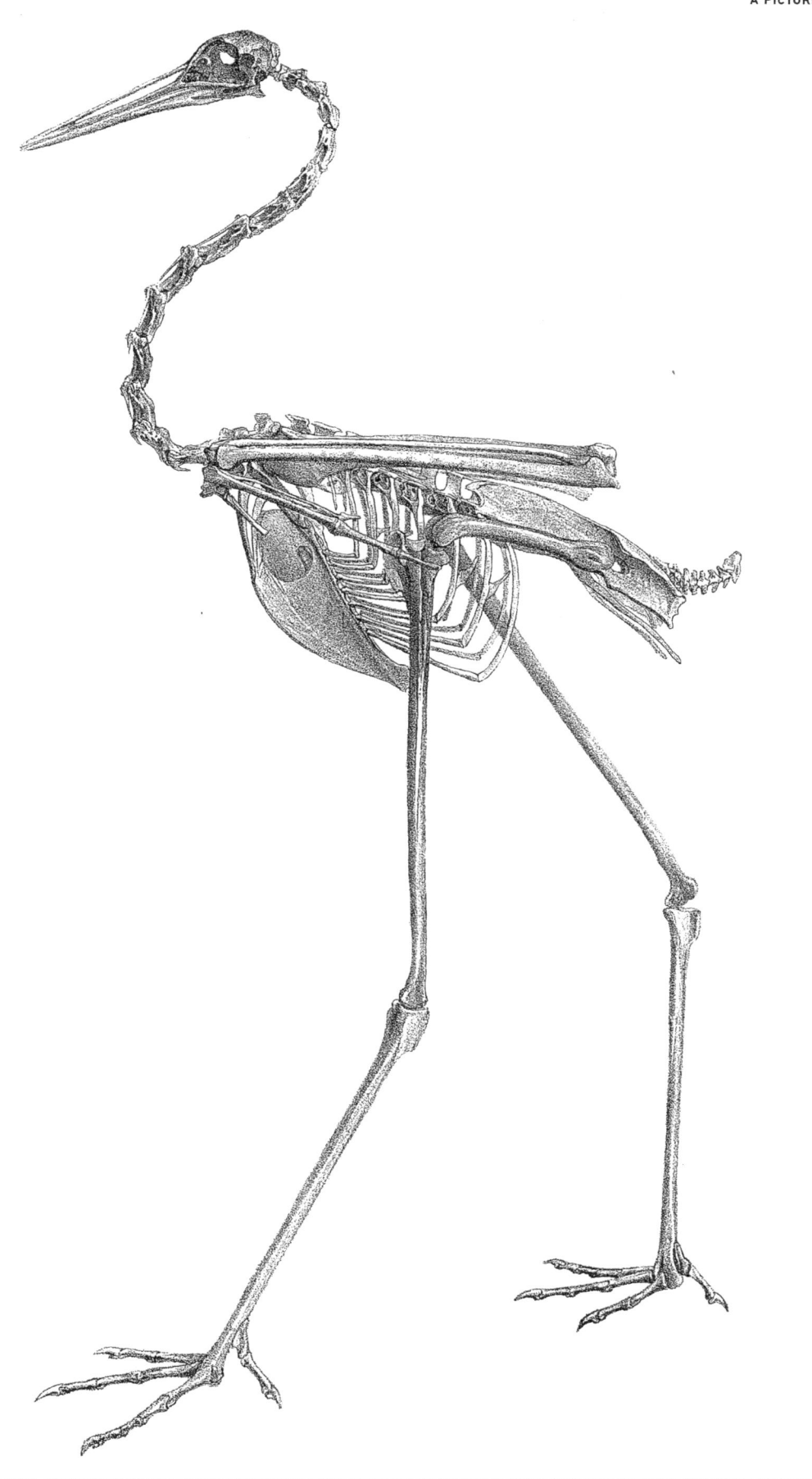

Fig.33 Ephippiorhynchus Senegalensis.

Fig.34 Didunculus Strigirostris.

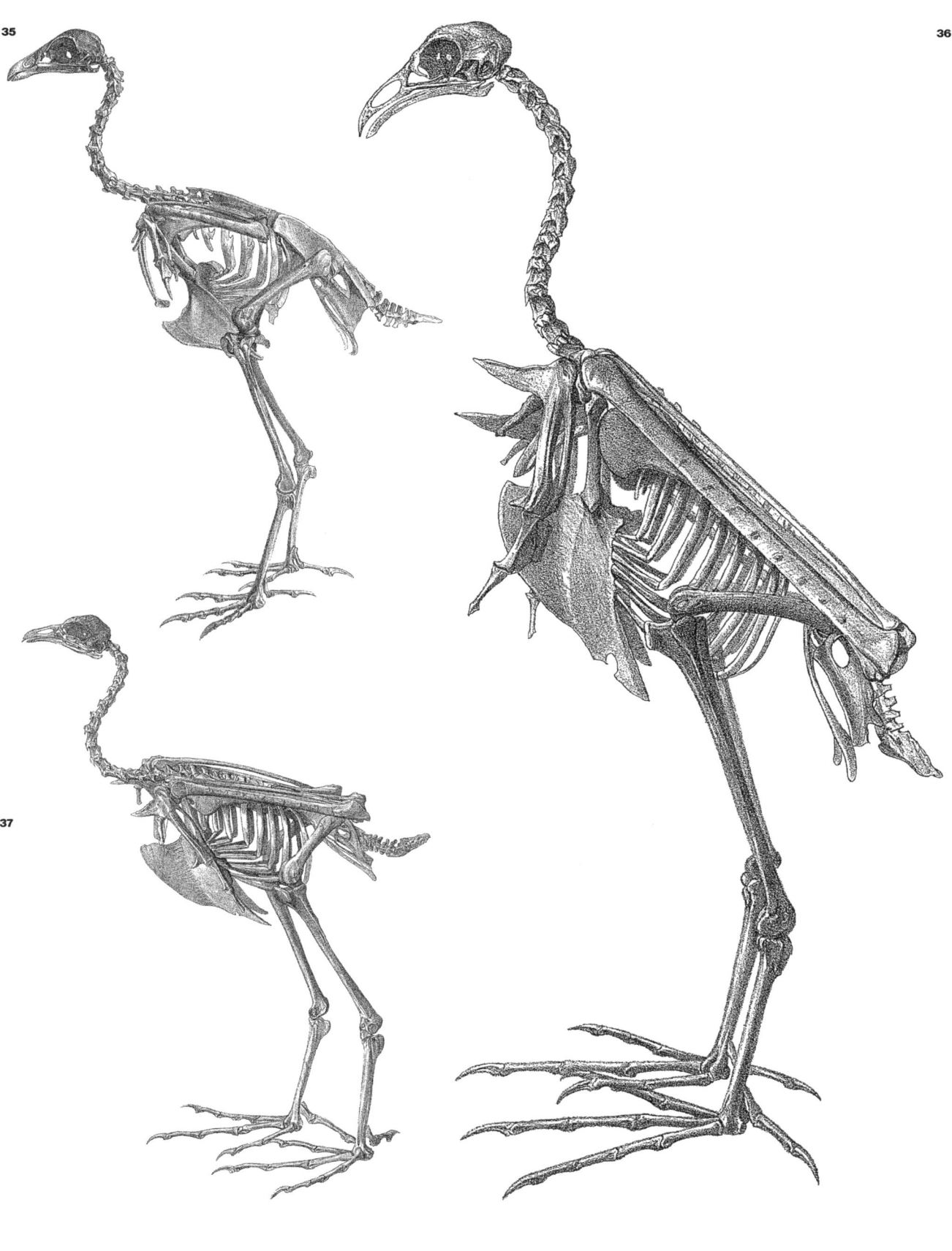

Fig.35 Tallegalla Lathami.

Fig.36 Palamedea Cornuta.

Fig.37 Chauna Chavaria.

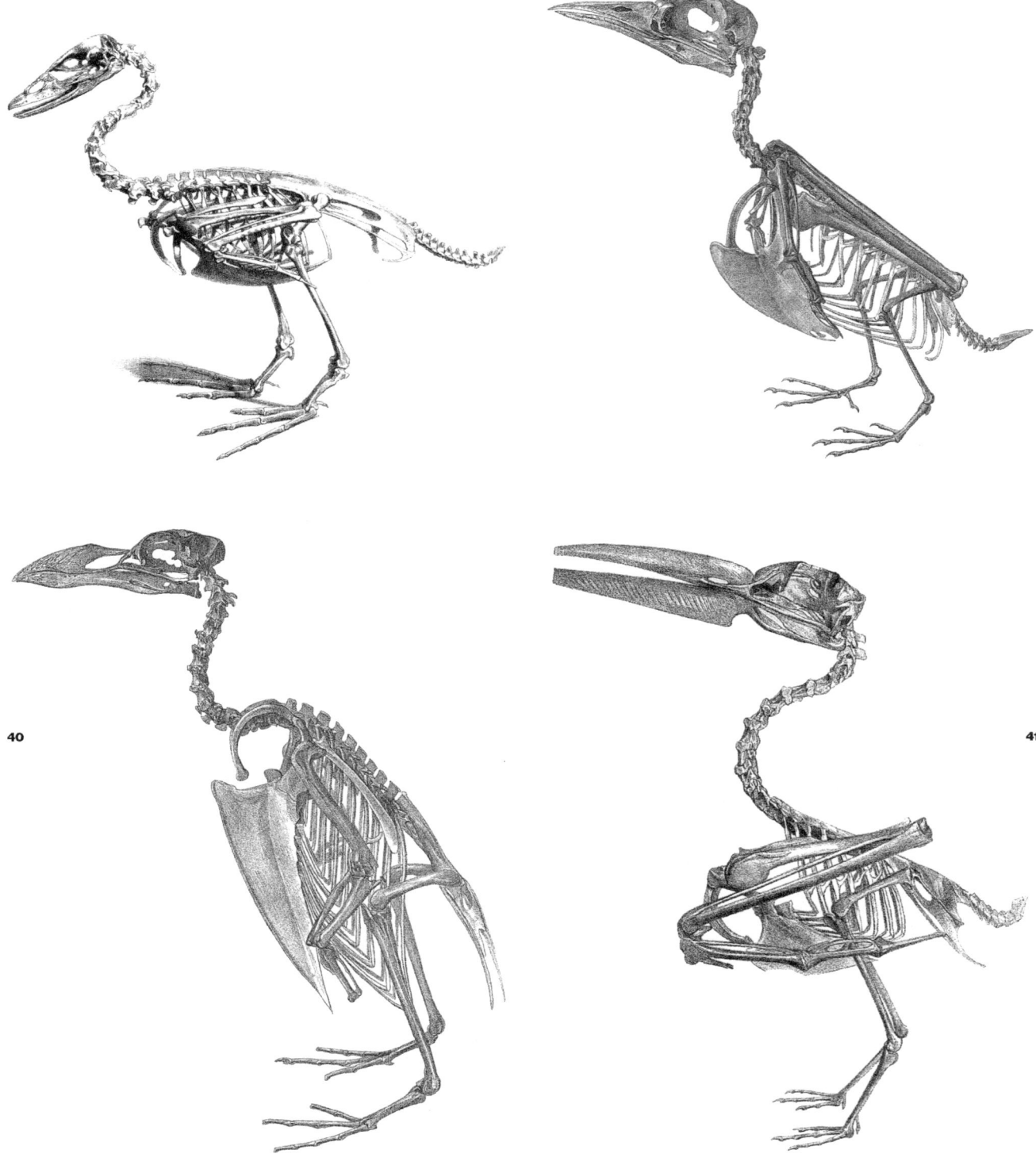

Fig.38 Biziura (Hydrobates) Lobatus.

Fig.39 Phaeton Ætherens.

Fig.40 Alca Impennis.

Fig.41 Rhynchops Nigra.

Fig.42 Chroicocephalus Ridibundus.

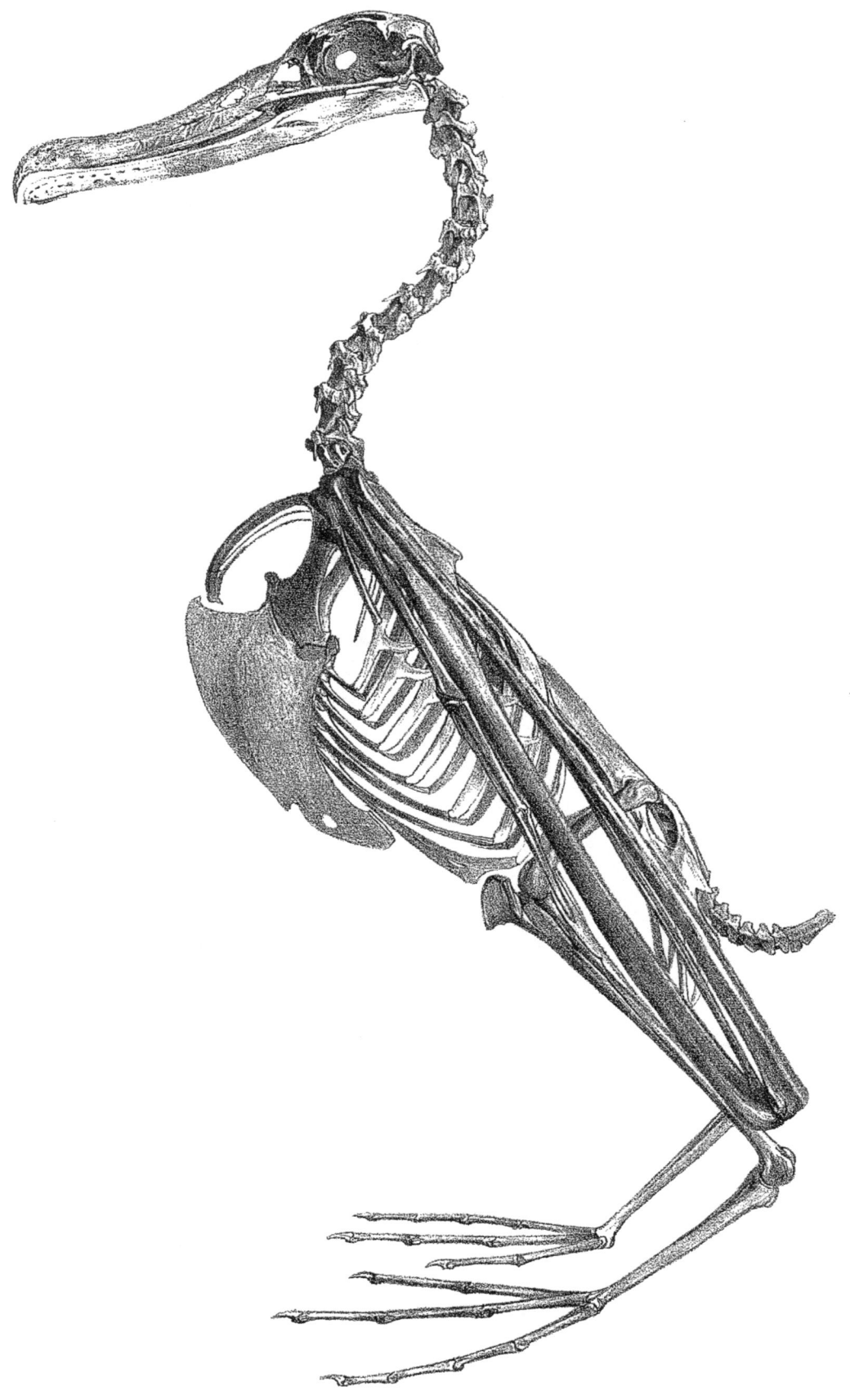

Fig.43 Diomedea Exulans.

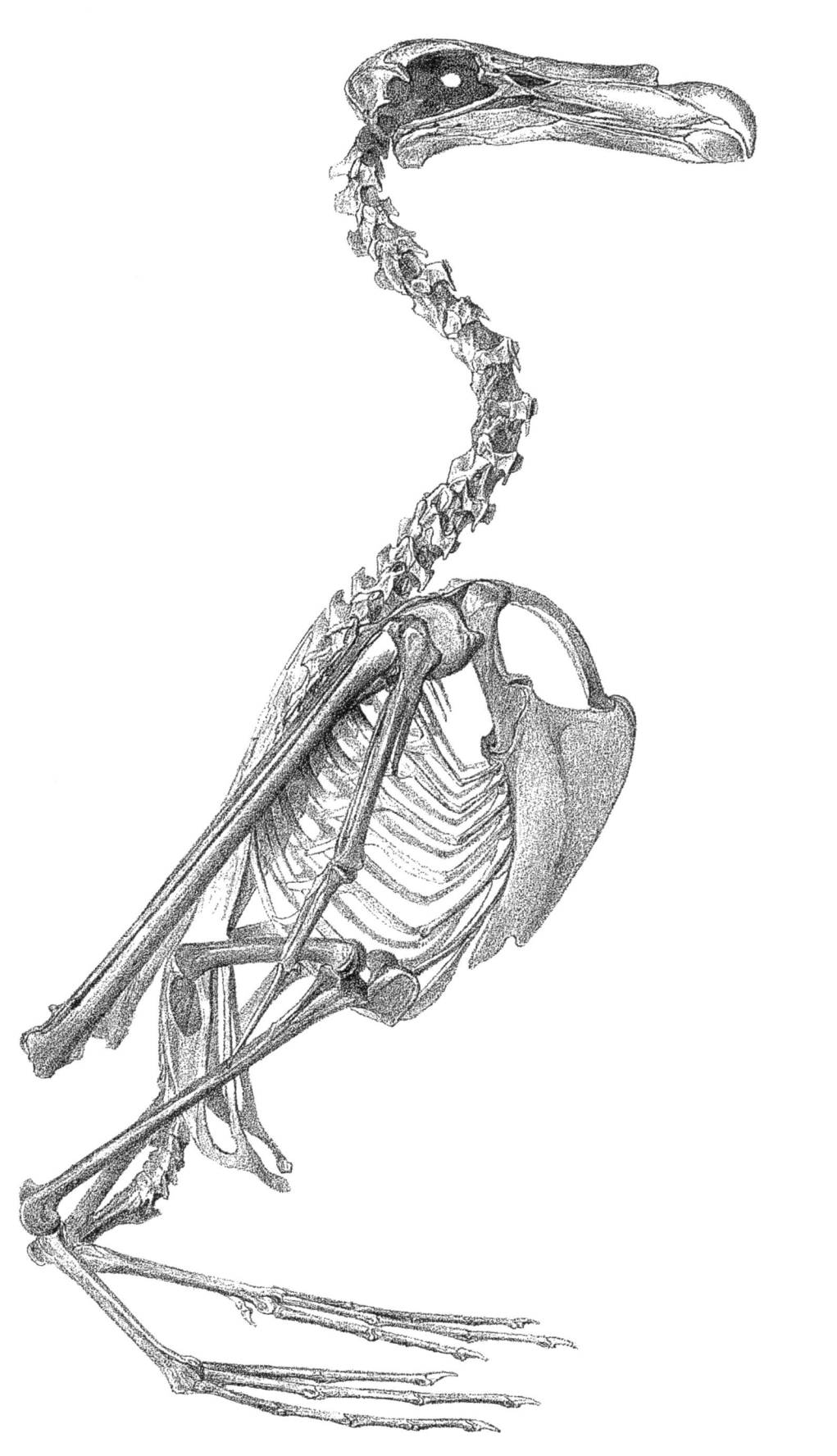

Fig.44 Procellaria Gigantia.

45

46

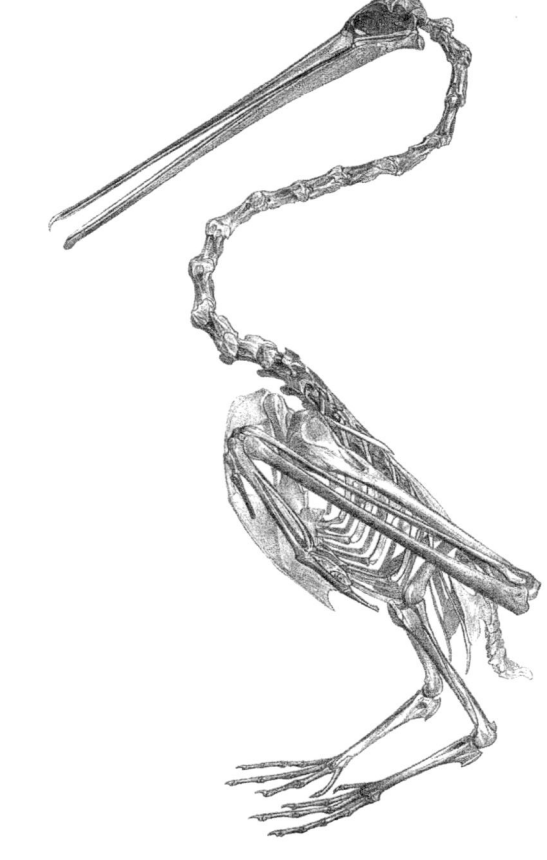

47

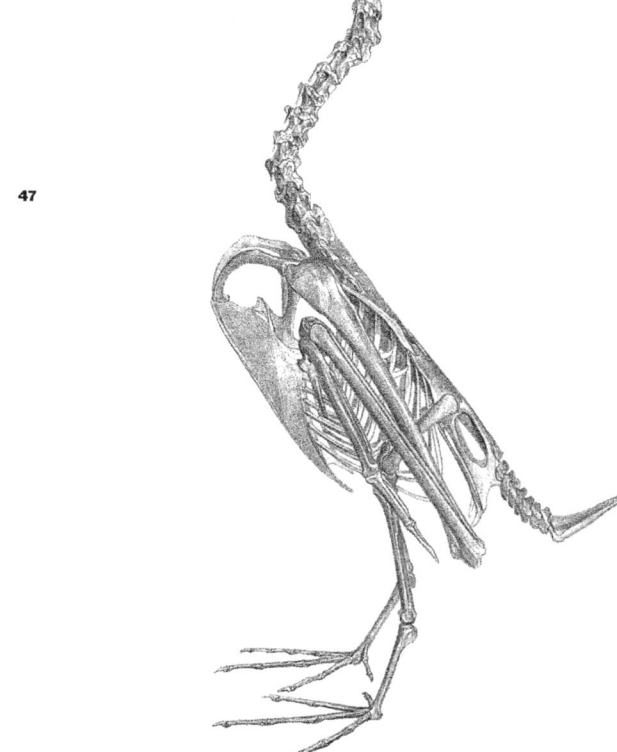

48

Fig.45 Thalassidroma Pelagica. Fig.46 Onocrotalus. Fig.47 Sola Basana. Fig.48 Eudyptes.

Fig.49 Graculus Christatus.

Fig.50 Uria Troile.

Fig.51 Podiceps Christatus.

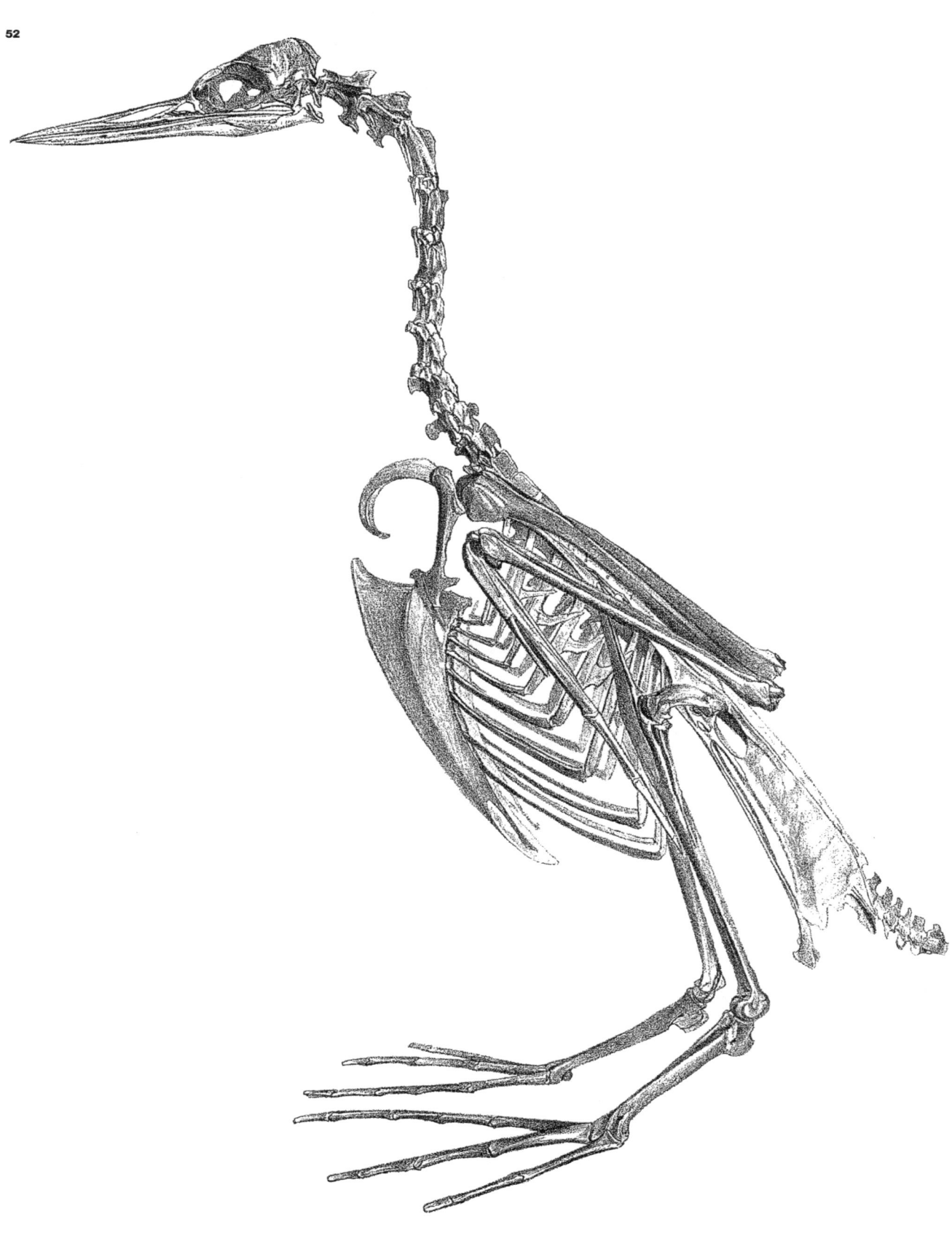

Fig.52 Colymbus Septentrionalis.

Fig.53 Œdicnemus Longirostris.

Fig.54 Aramus Scolopaceus.

Fig.55 Glareola Pratincola.

Fig.56 Helias Phalenoides.

57

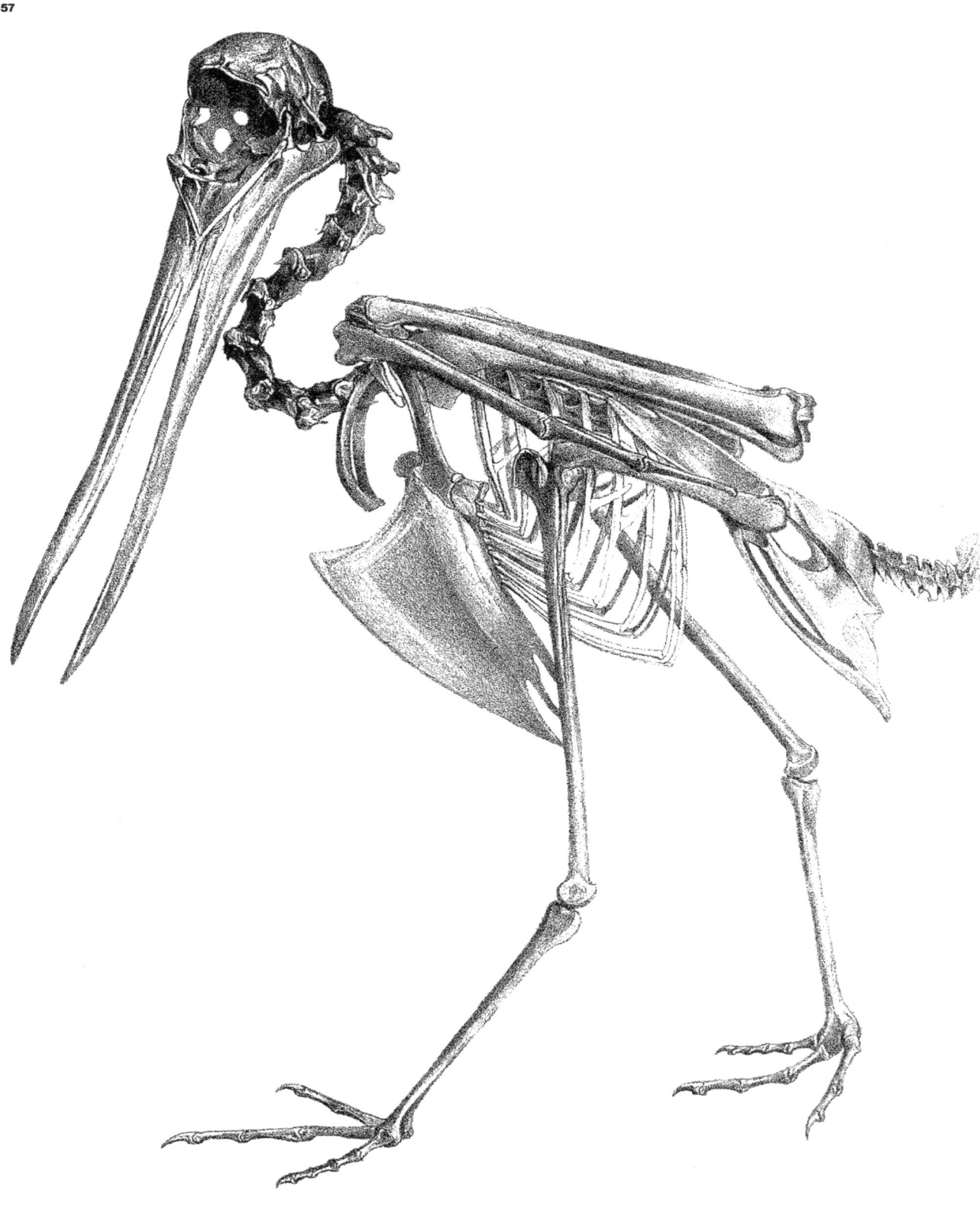

Fig.57 V

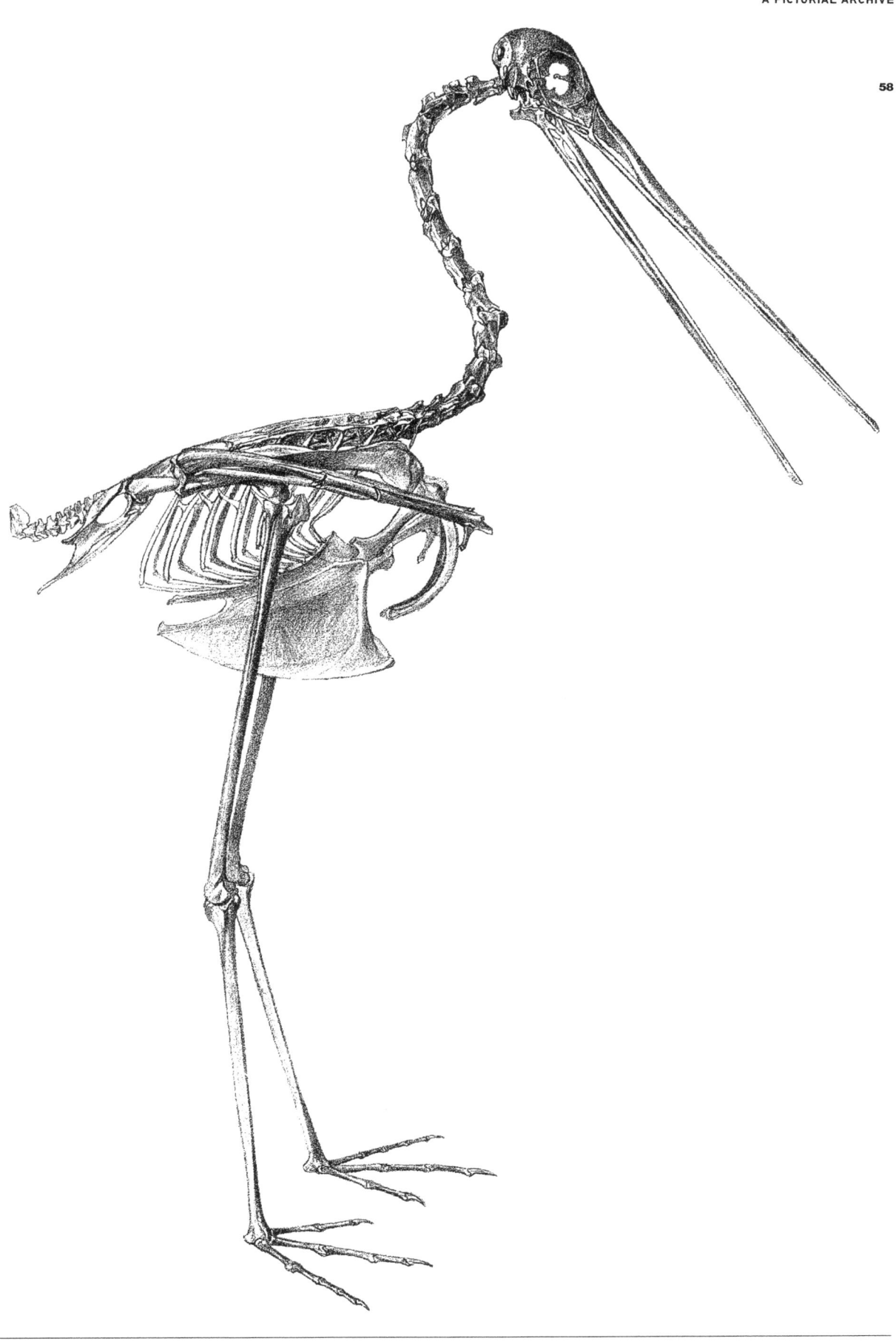

Fig.58 Limosa Rufa.

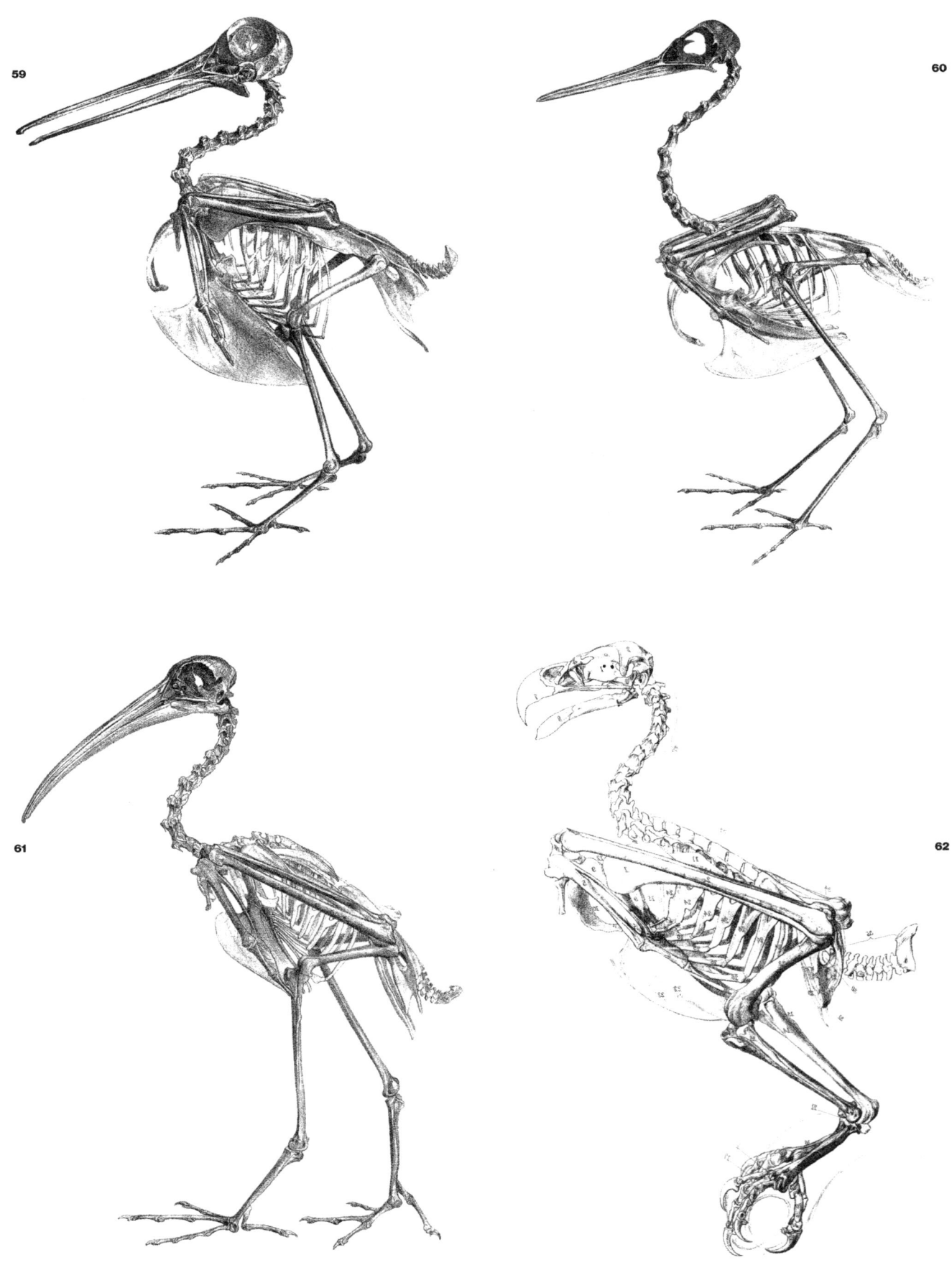

Fig.59 Scolopax Rusticola.

Fig.60 Totanus Glottis.

Fig.61 Harpiprion Hagedacch.

Fig.62 Pandion Leucocephalus.

Fig.63 Treskionis Melanocephala.

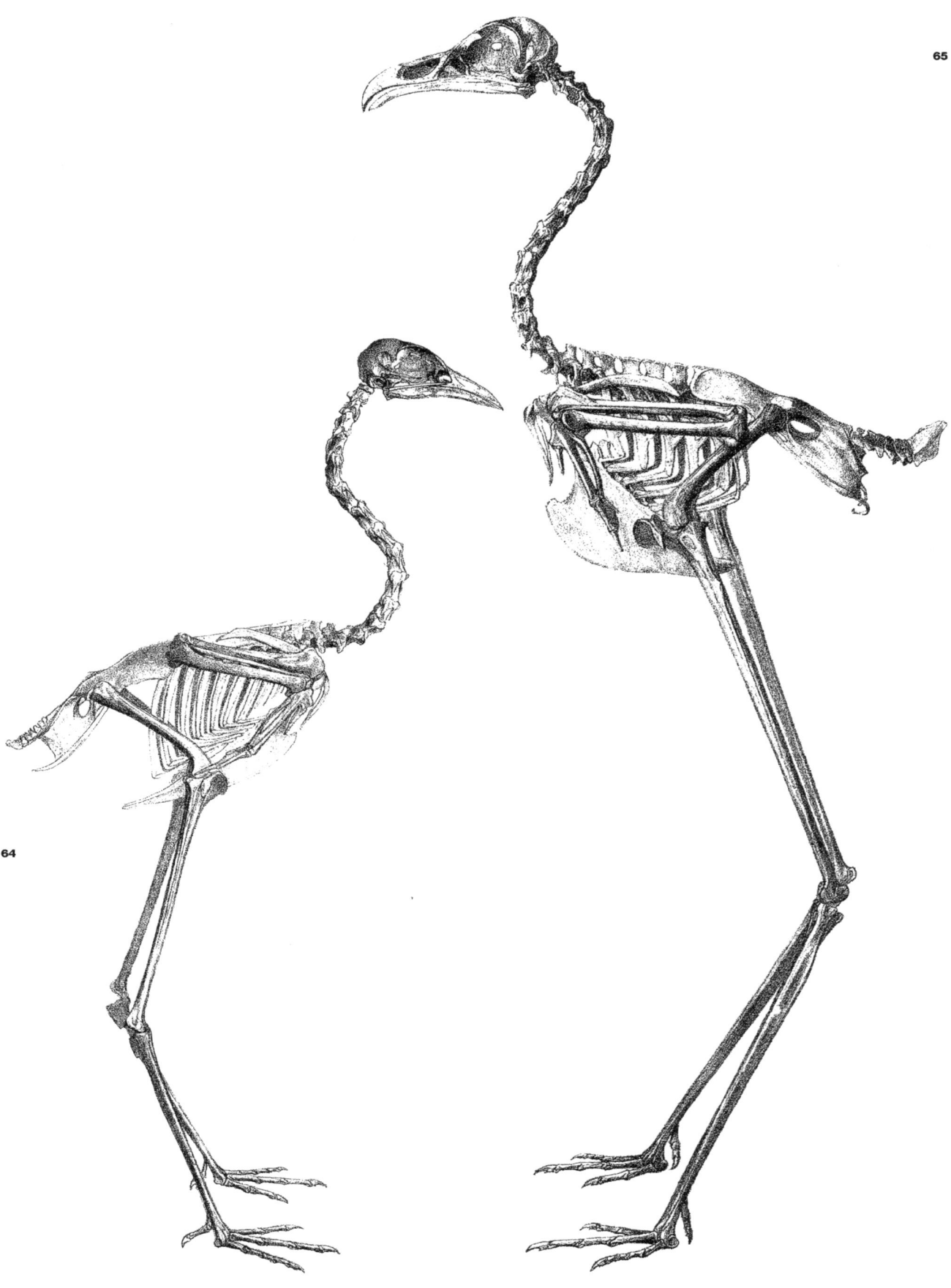

Fig.64 Psophia Viridis.

Fig.65 Cariama Cristata.

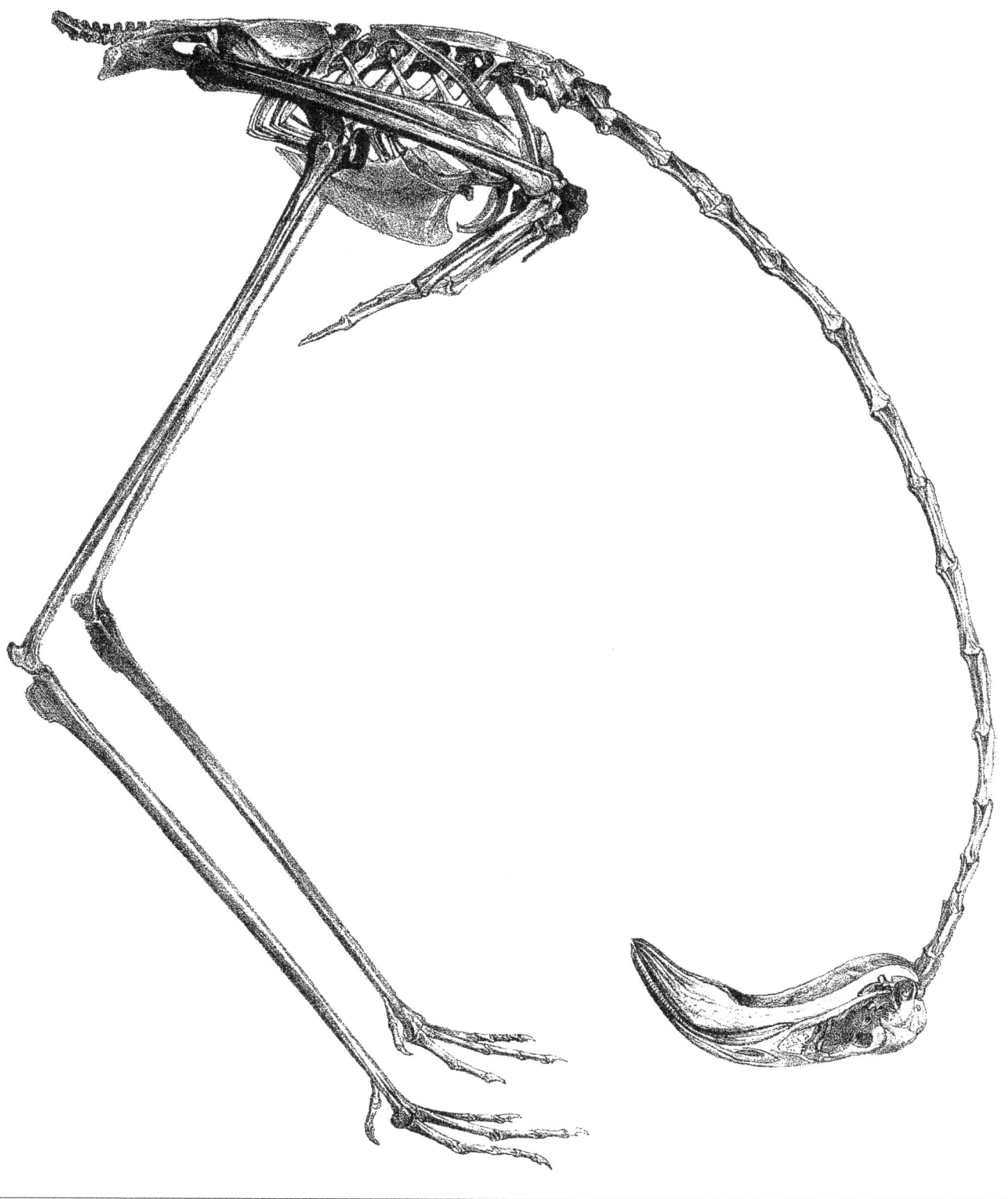

Fig.66 Phœnicopterus Ruber.

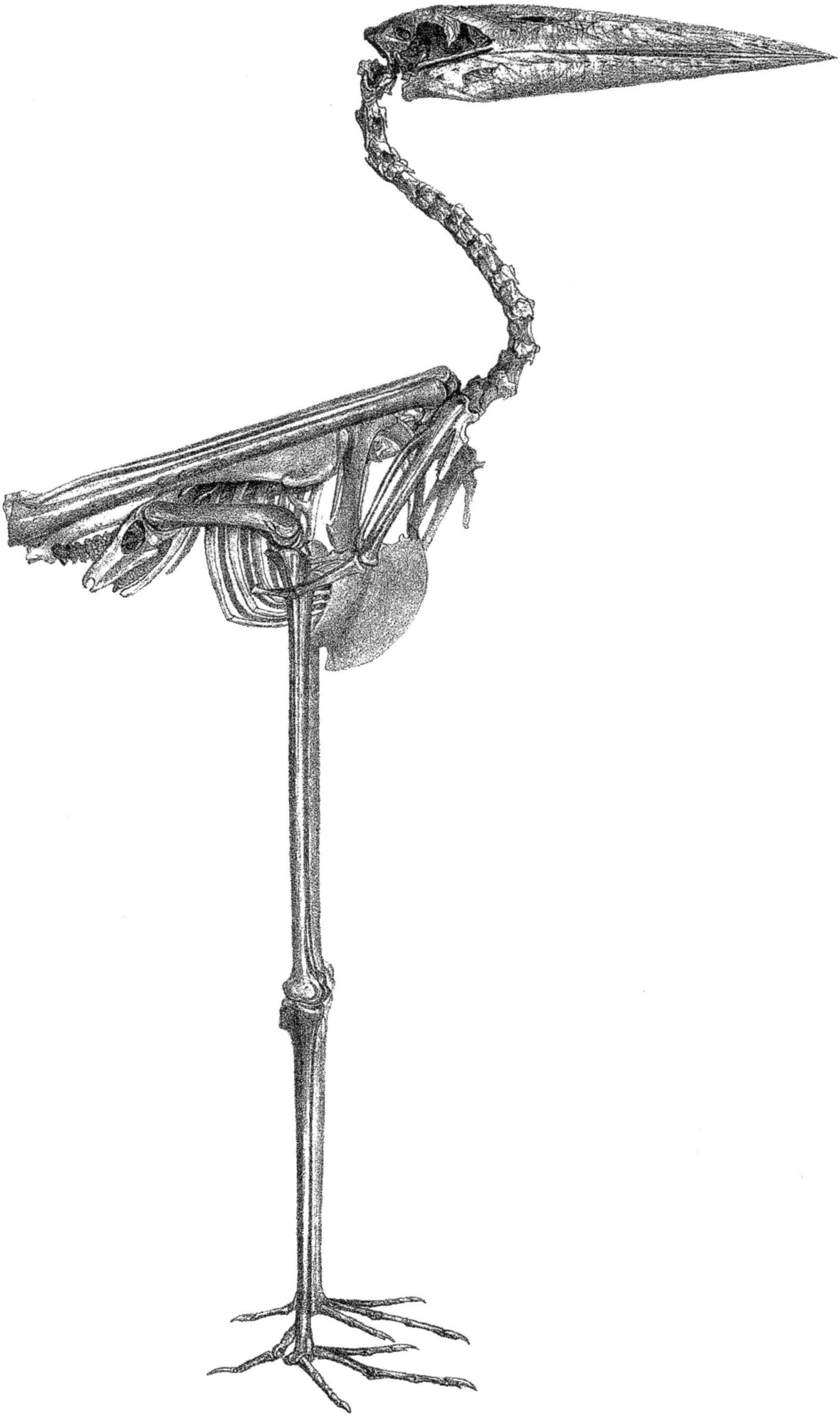

Fig.67 Leptophilus
Argala.

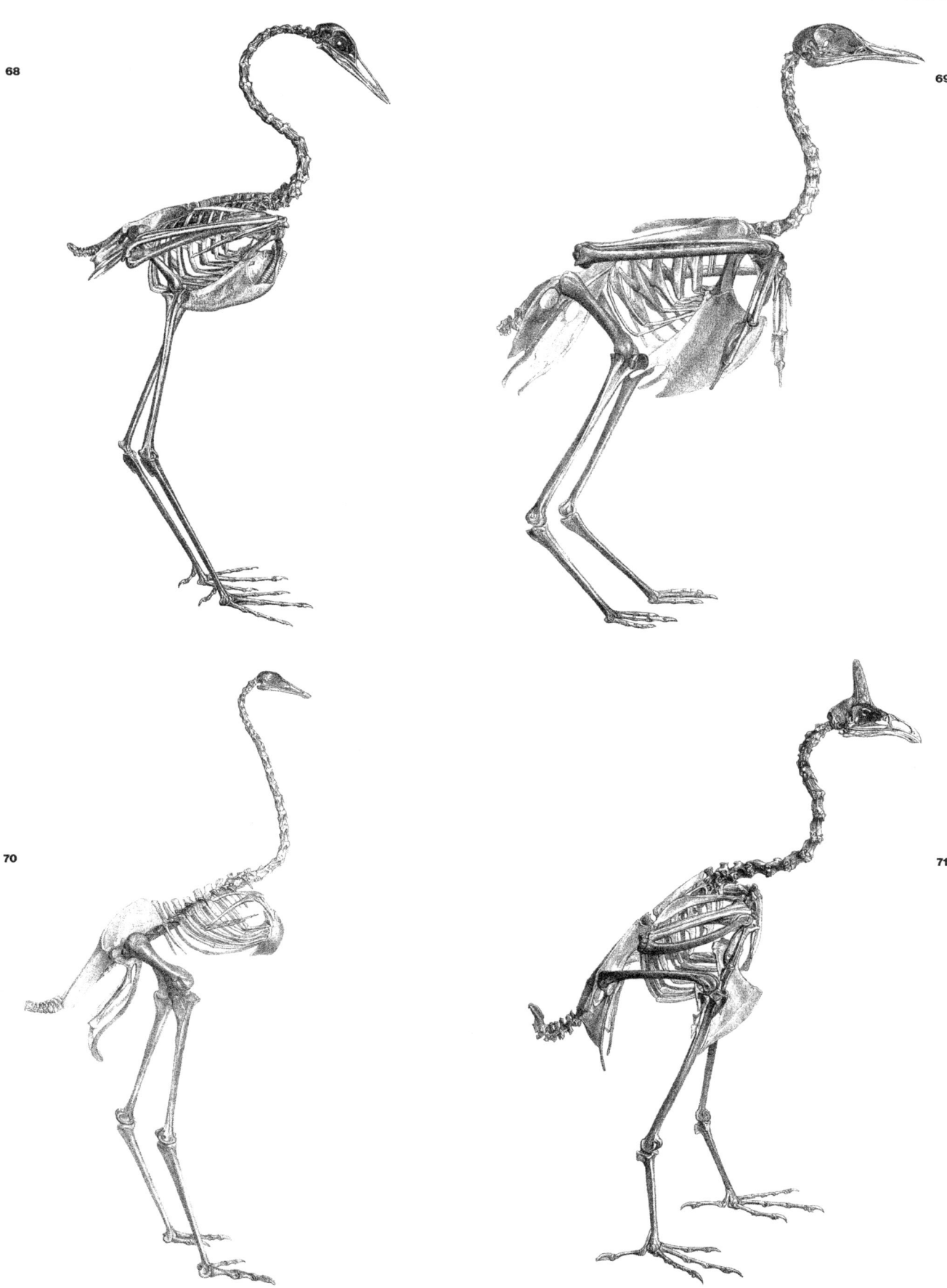

Fig.68 Scops Virgo.
Fig.69 Otis Houbara.
Fig.70 Struthio Camelus.
Fig.71 Oreophasis Derbyanus.

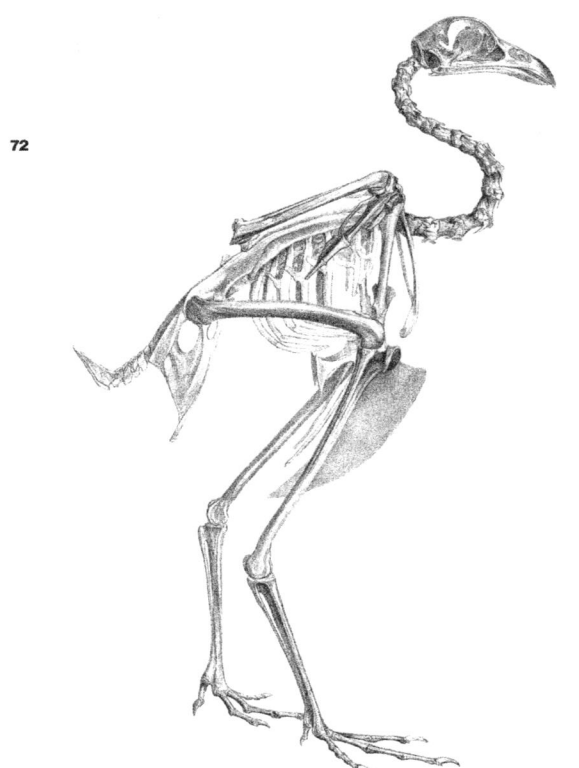

Fig.72 Phasianus Nycthemerus.

Fig.73 Crax Globicera.

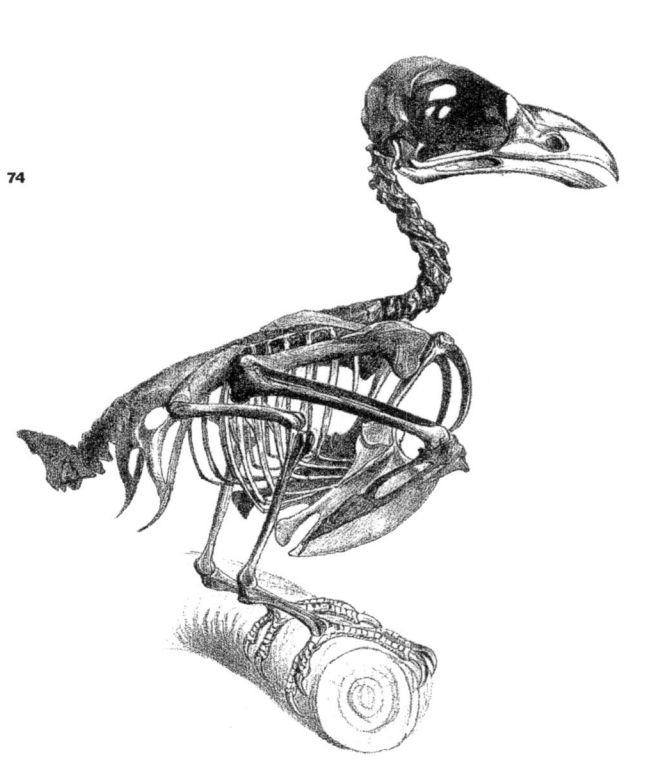

Fig.74 Trogon Melanocephalus.

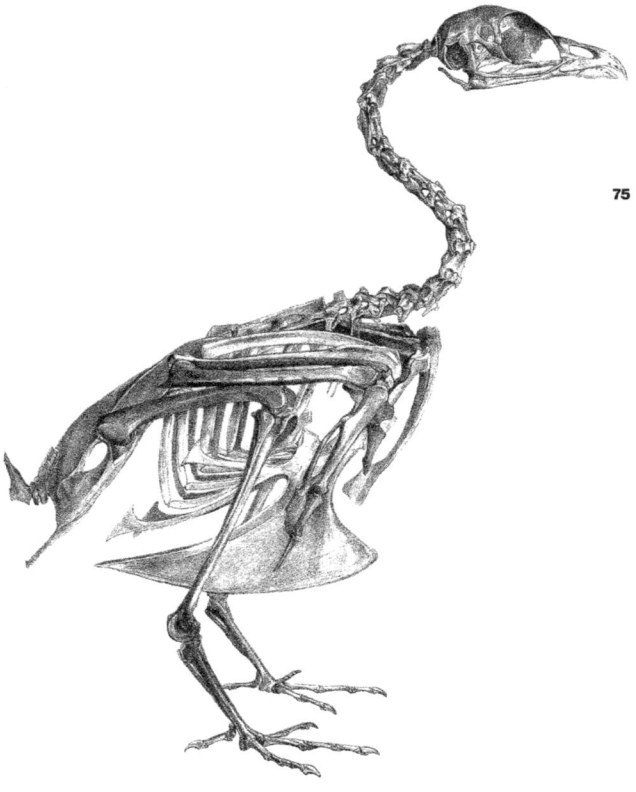

Fig.75 Tetrao Urogallus.

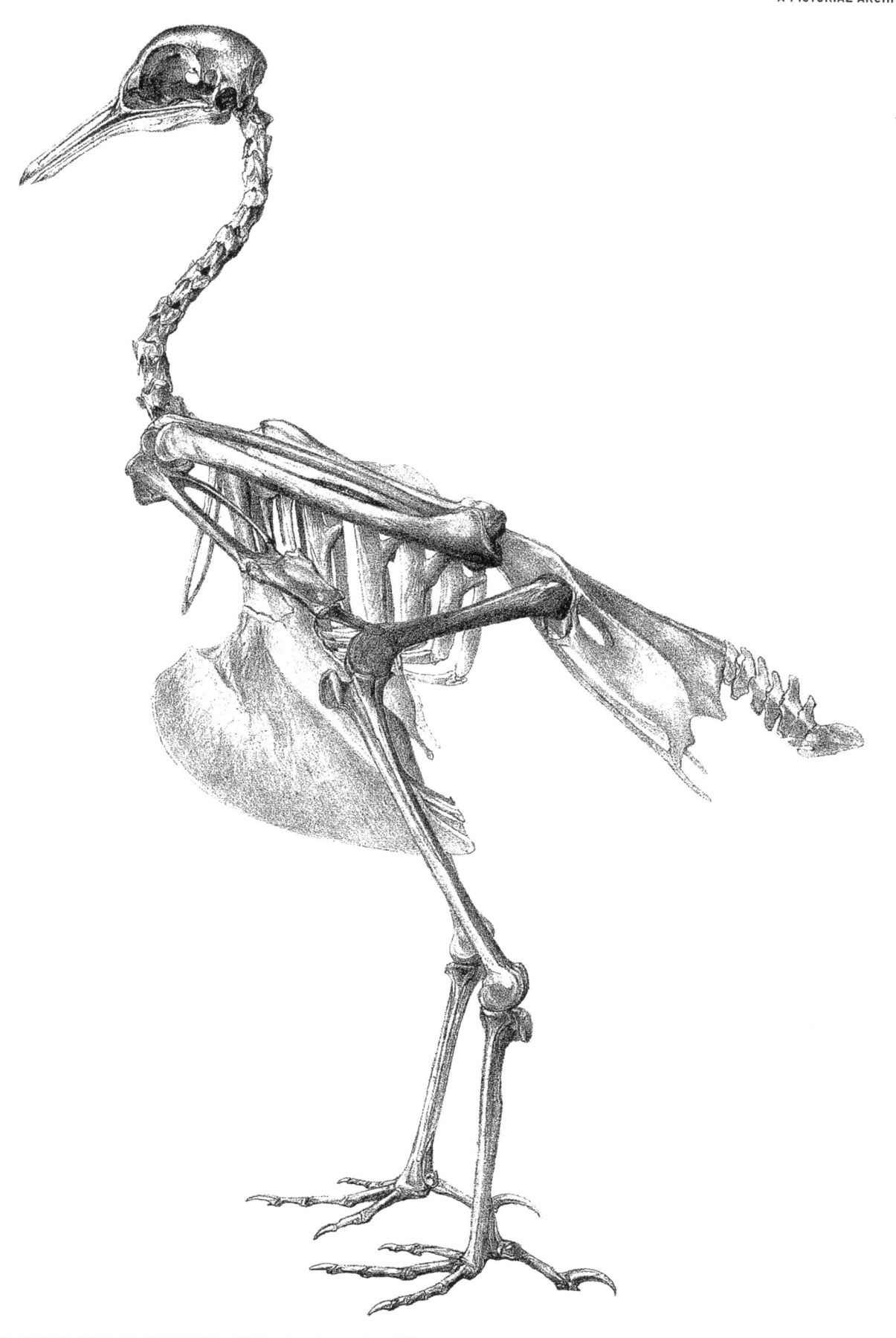

Fig.76 Goura Coronata.

Fig.77 Cypsirhina Leucoptera.

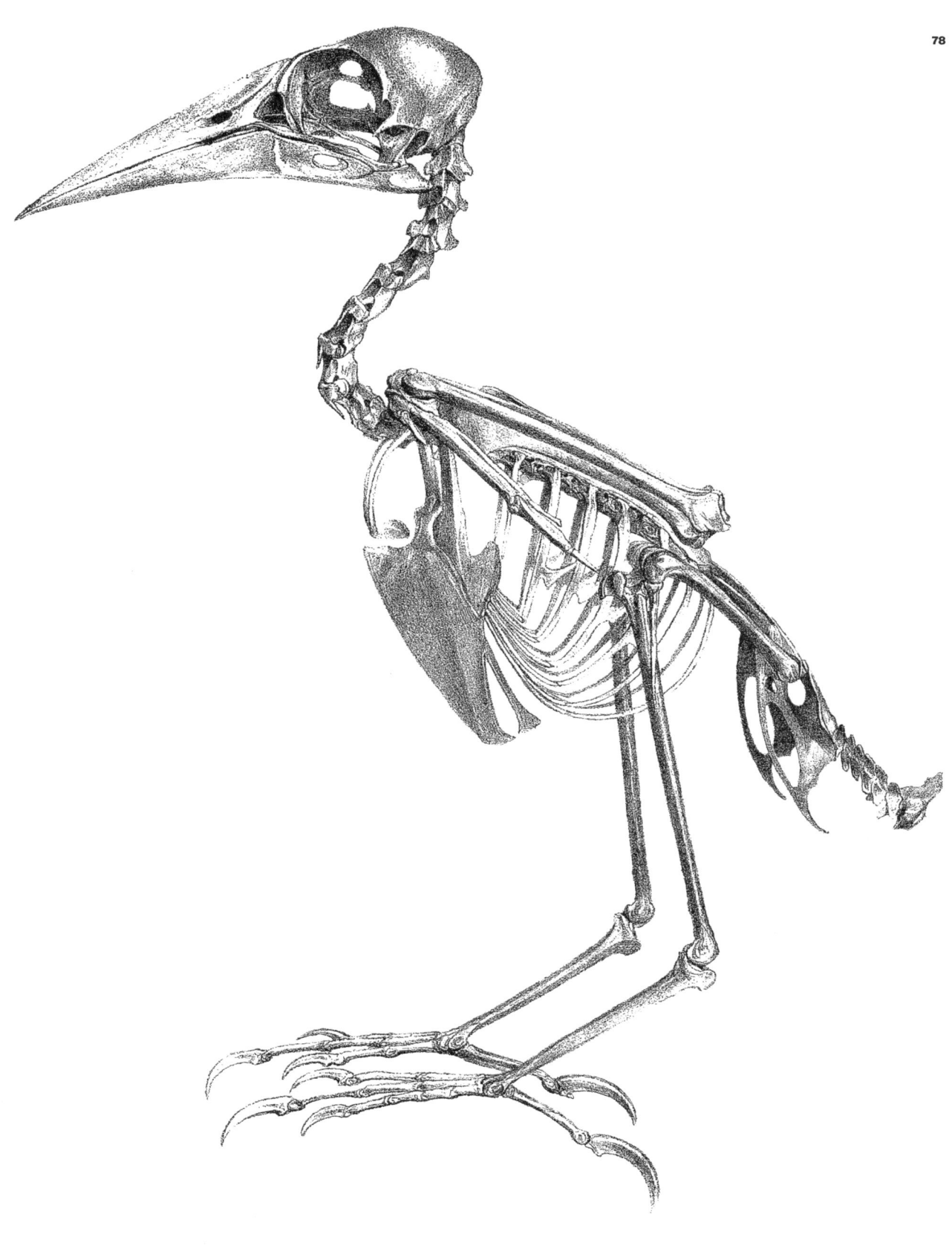

Fig.78 Cassicus Bifasciatus.

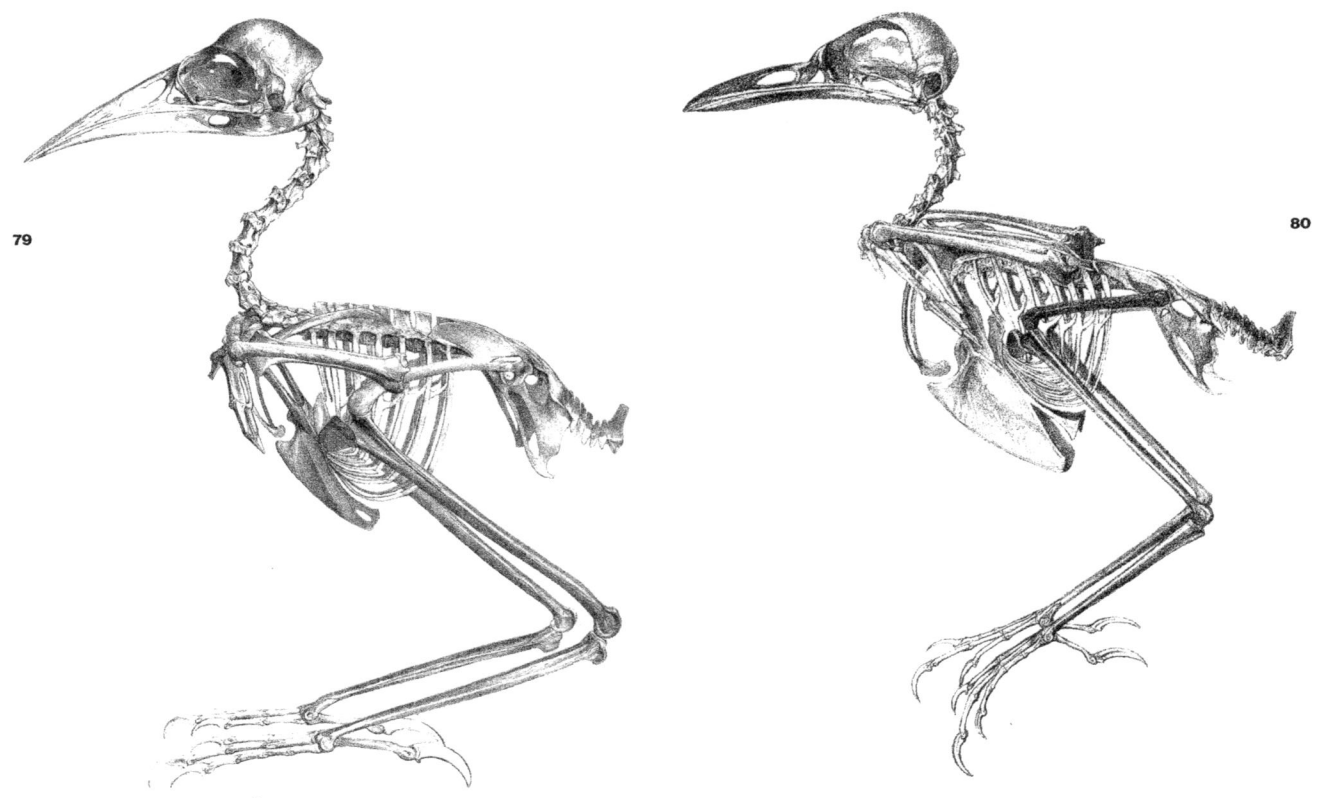
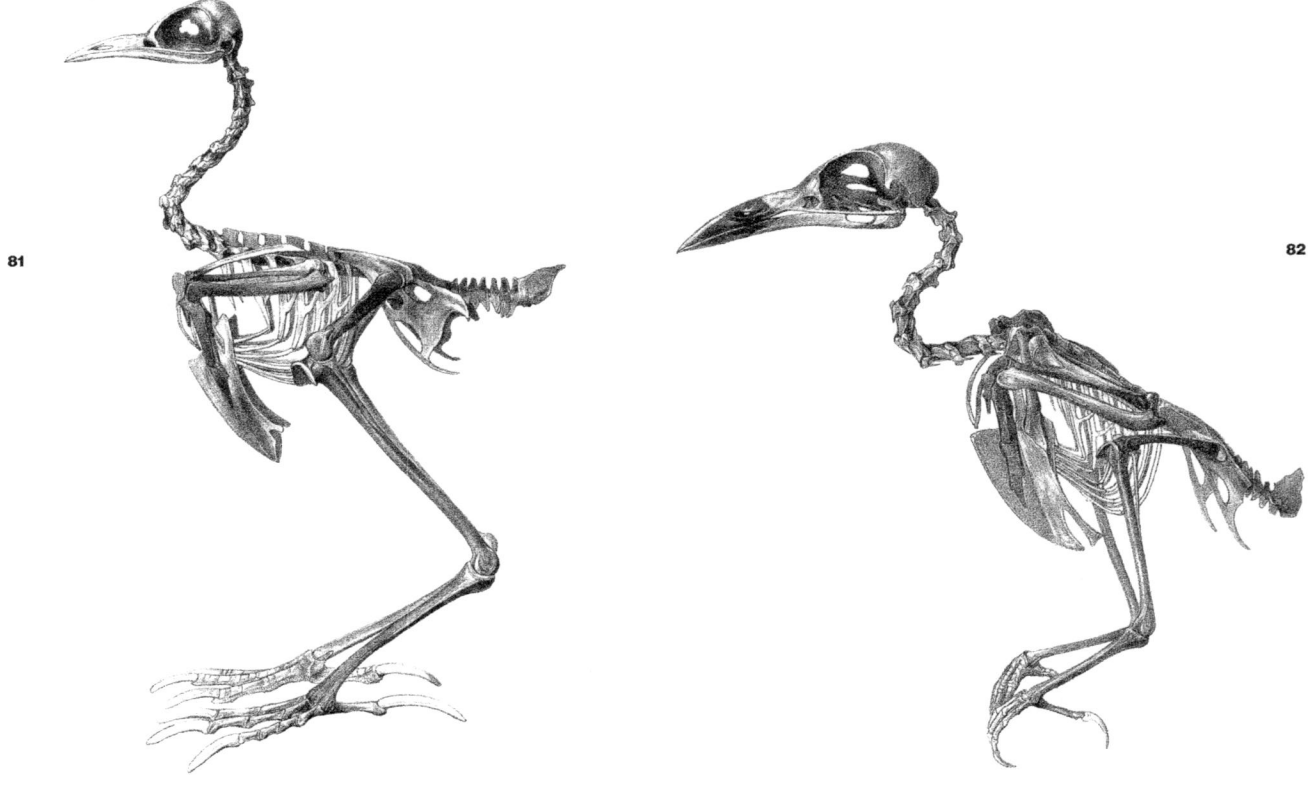

Fig.79 Neomorpha Gouldii.

Fig.80 Turdus Choki.

Fig.81 Menura Lyra.

Fig.82 Amthochæra Lewinii.

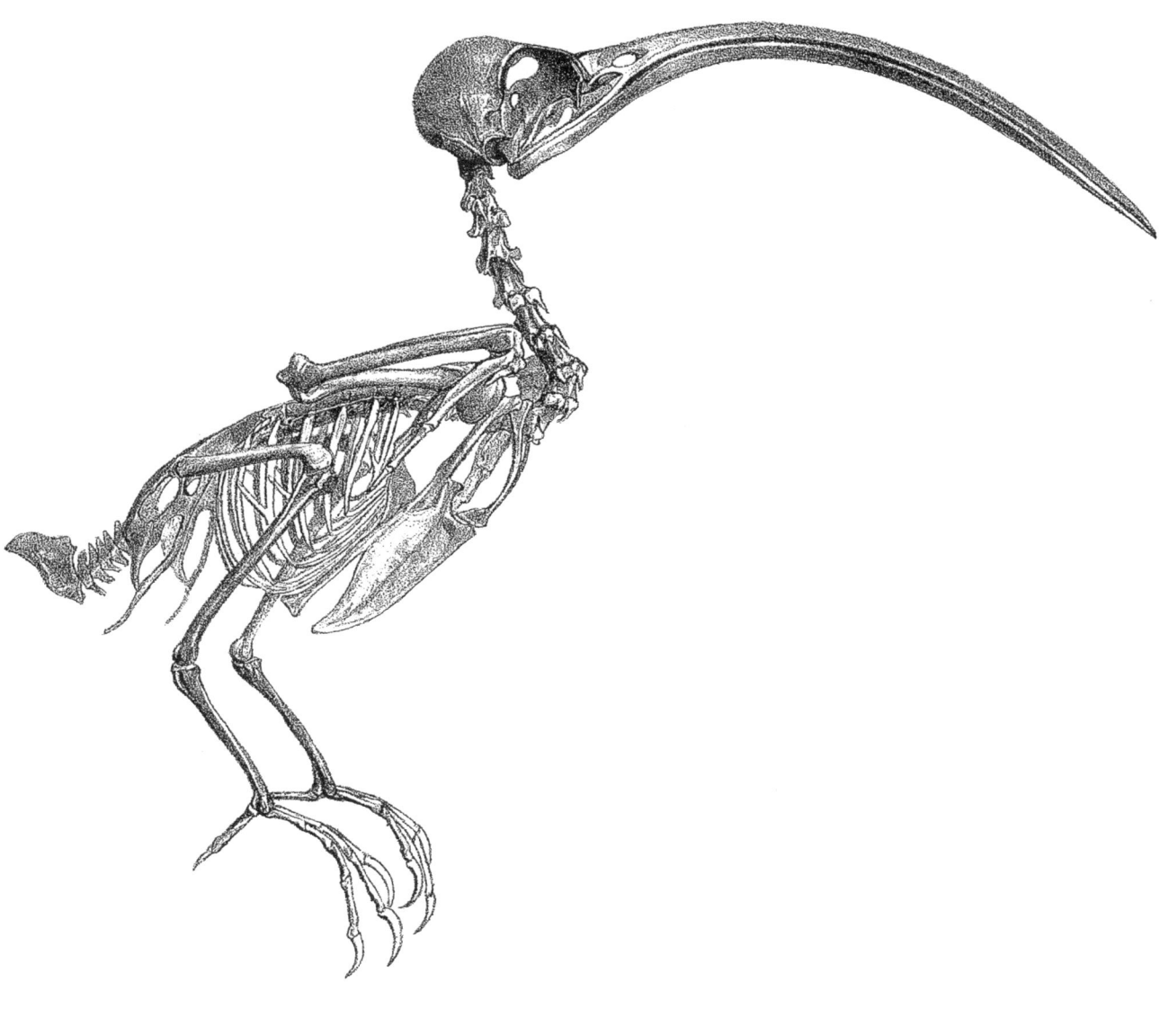

Fig.83 Ziphorhynchus
Trochilirostris.

Fig.84 Geococcyx Mexicanus.

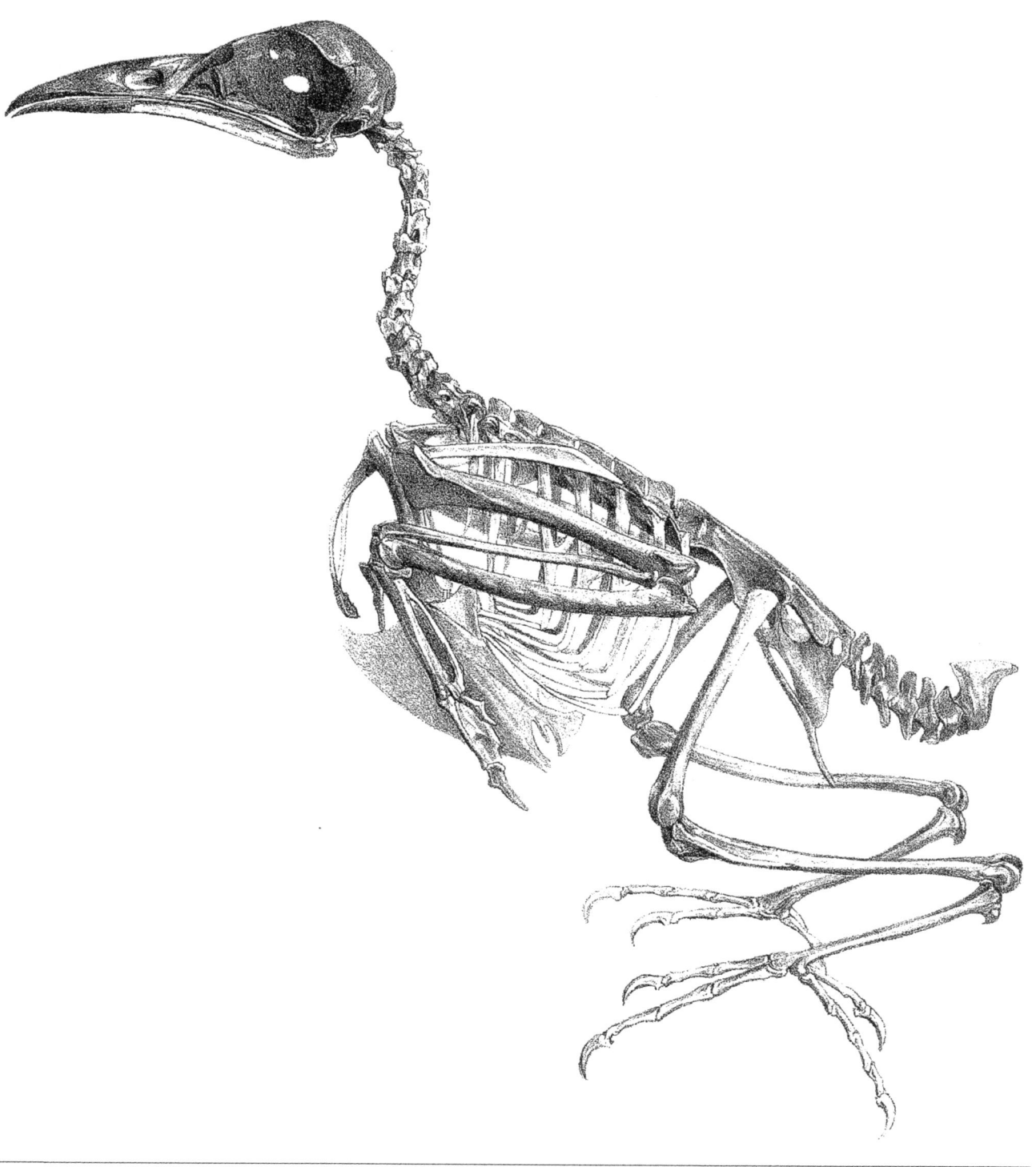

Fig.85 Cuculus
Glandarius.

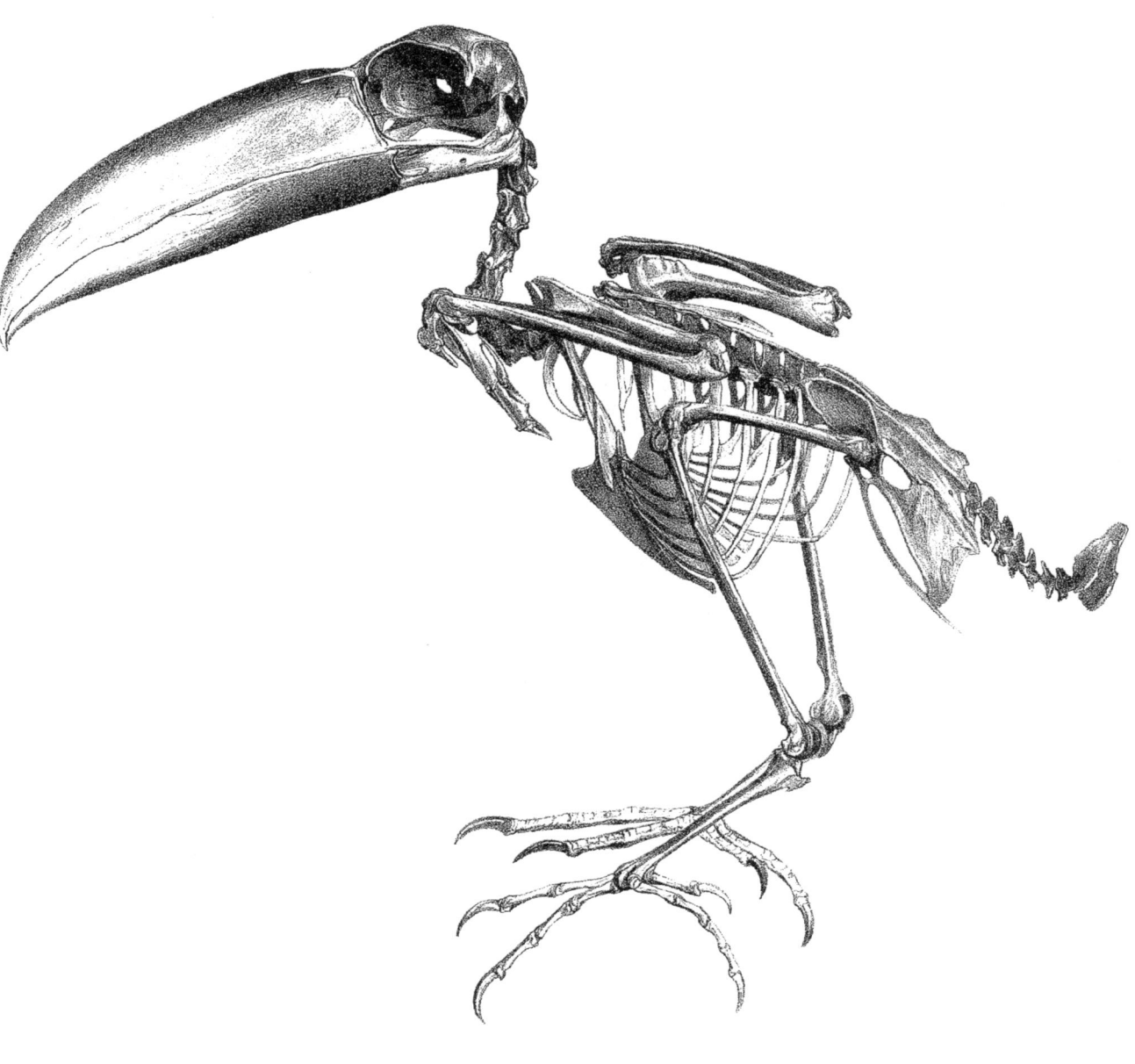

Fig.86 Pteroglossus Baillonii.

Fig.87 Turacus Gigas.

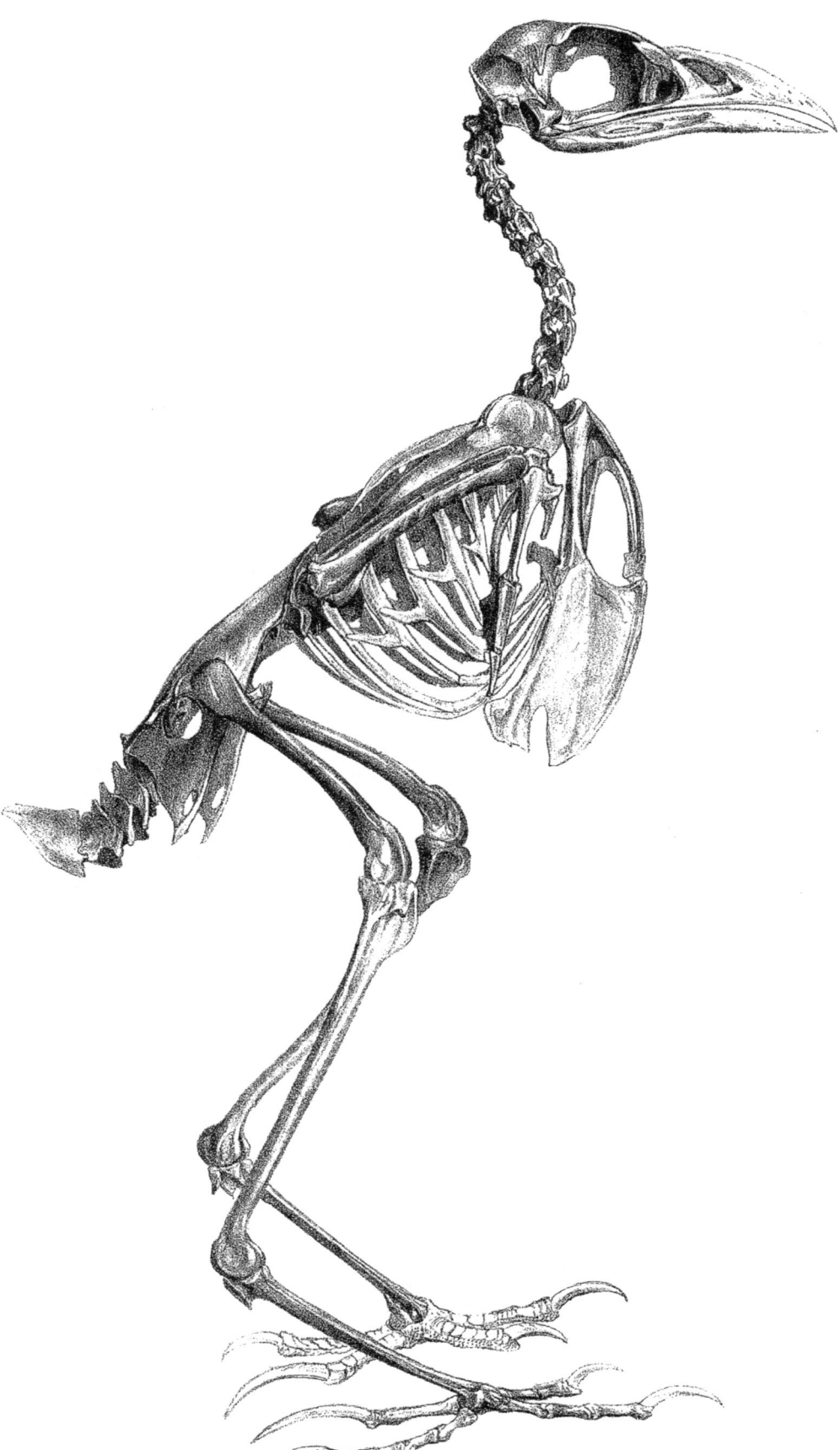

Fig.88 Centropus Phasianus.

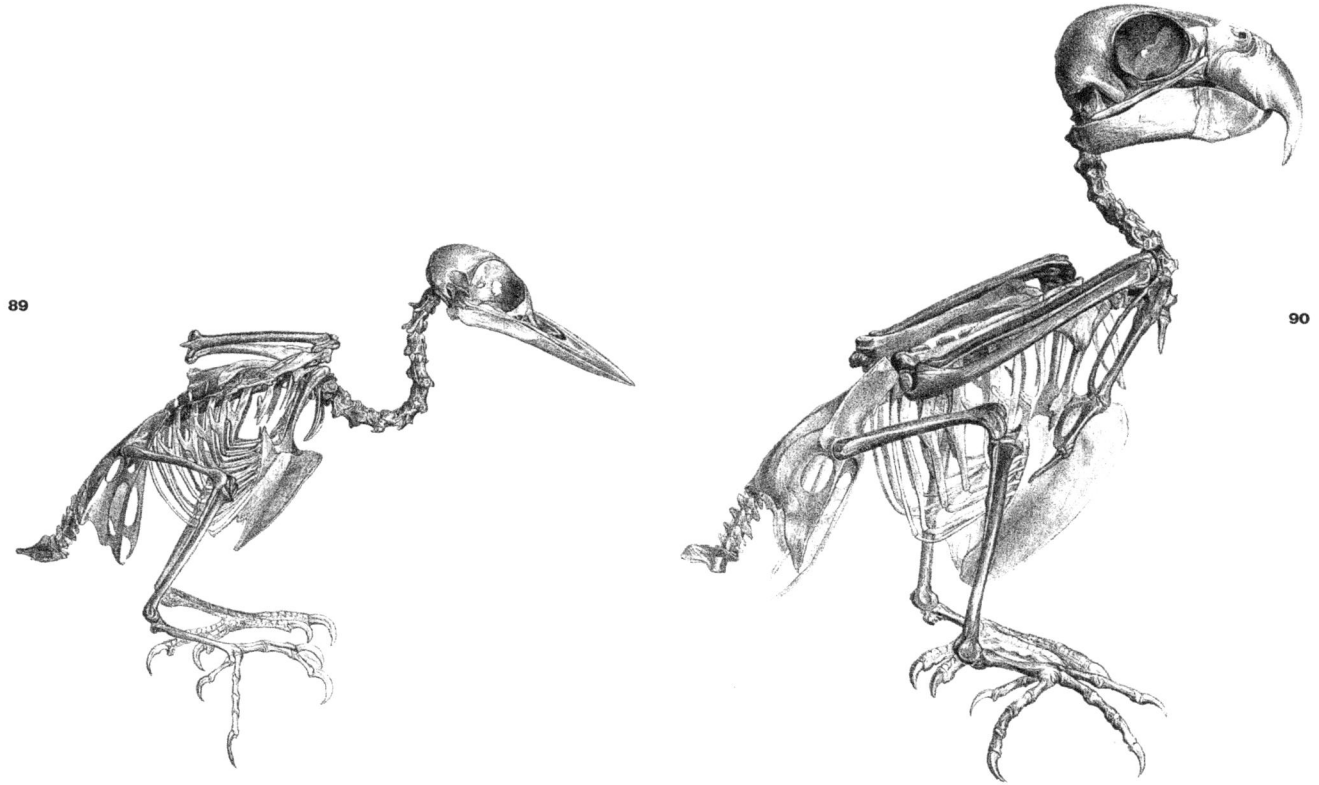
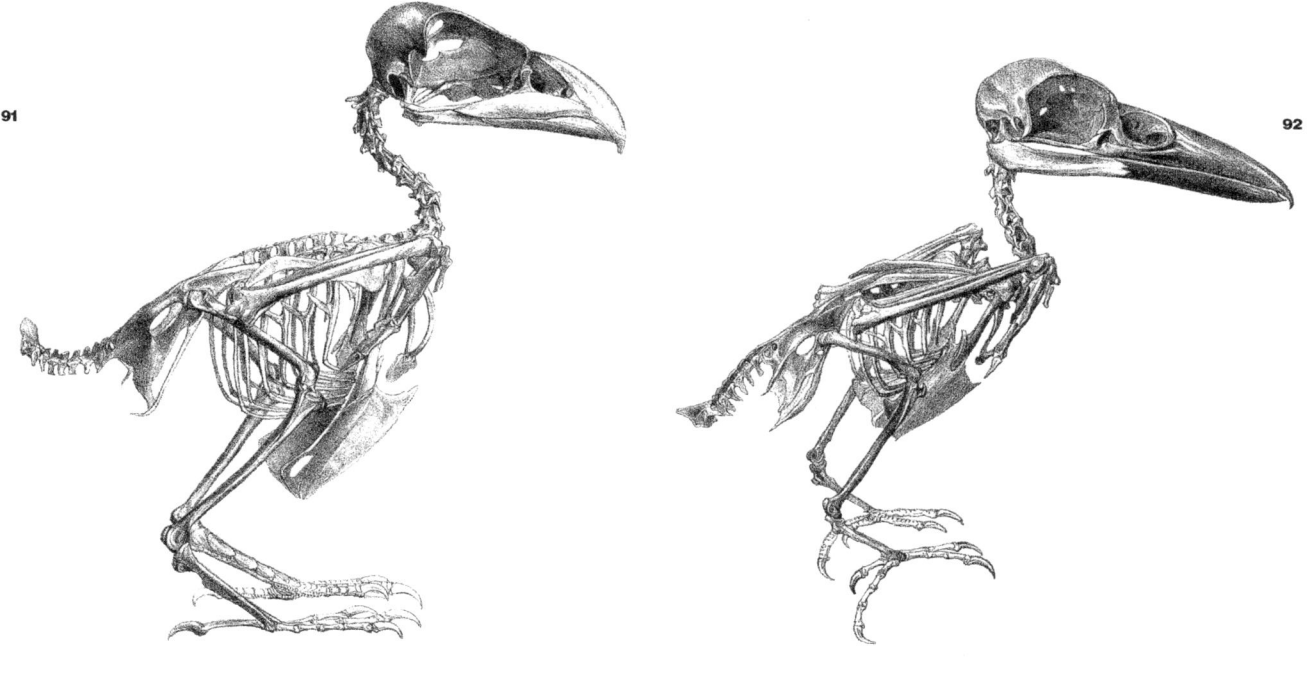

Fig.89 Gecinus Dimidiatus.

Fig.90 Chrysotis Braziliensis.

Fig.91 Eurylaimus Sumatranus.

Fig.92 Capito Swainsonii.

Fig.93 Buceros Abyssinicus.

Fig.94 Coracias Indica.

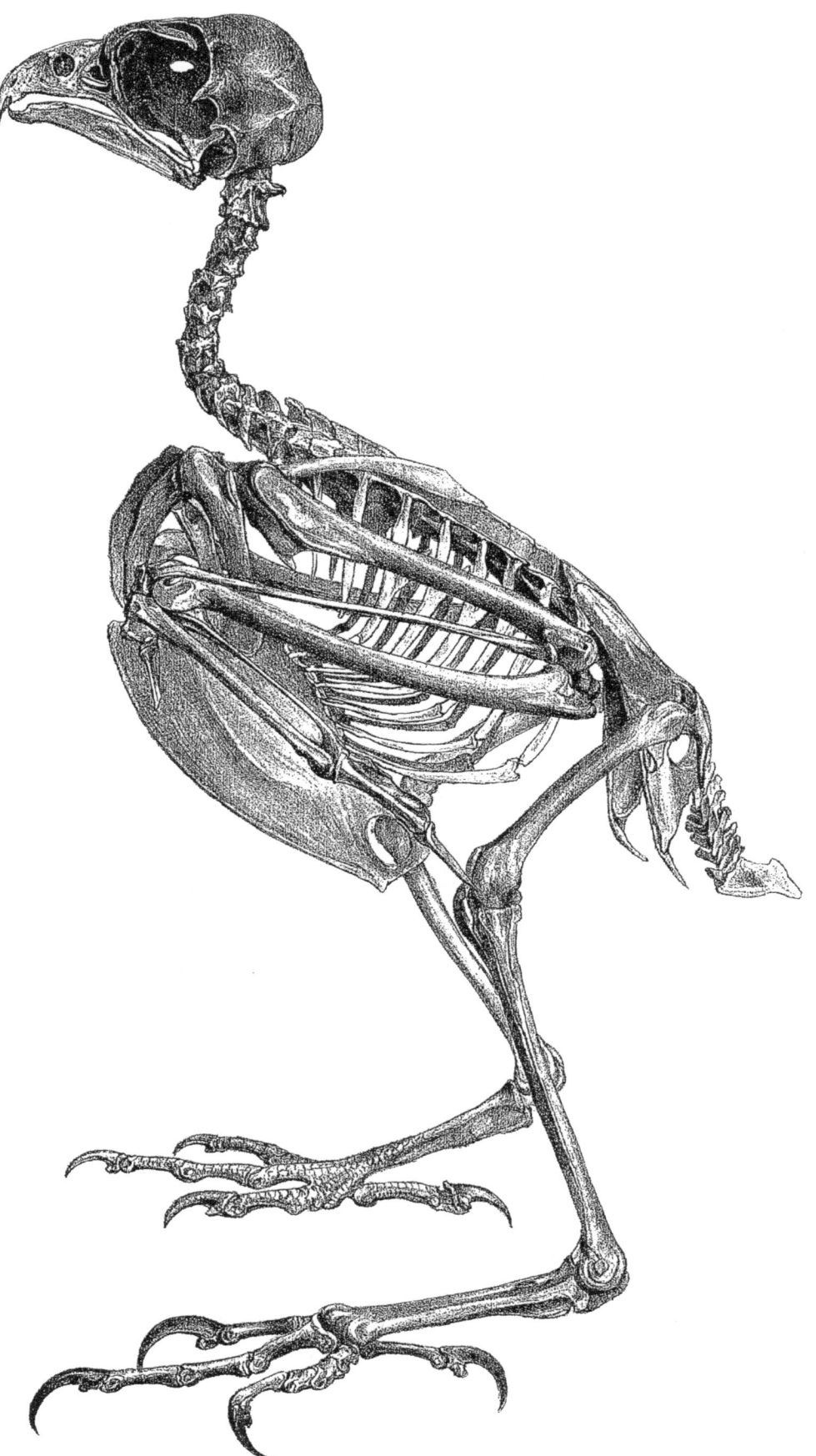

Fig.95 Falco Peregrinus.

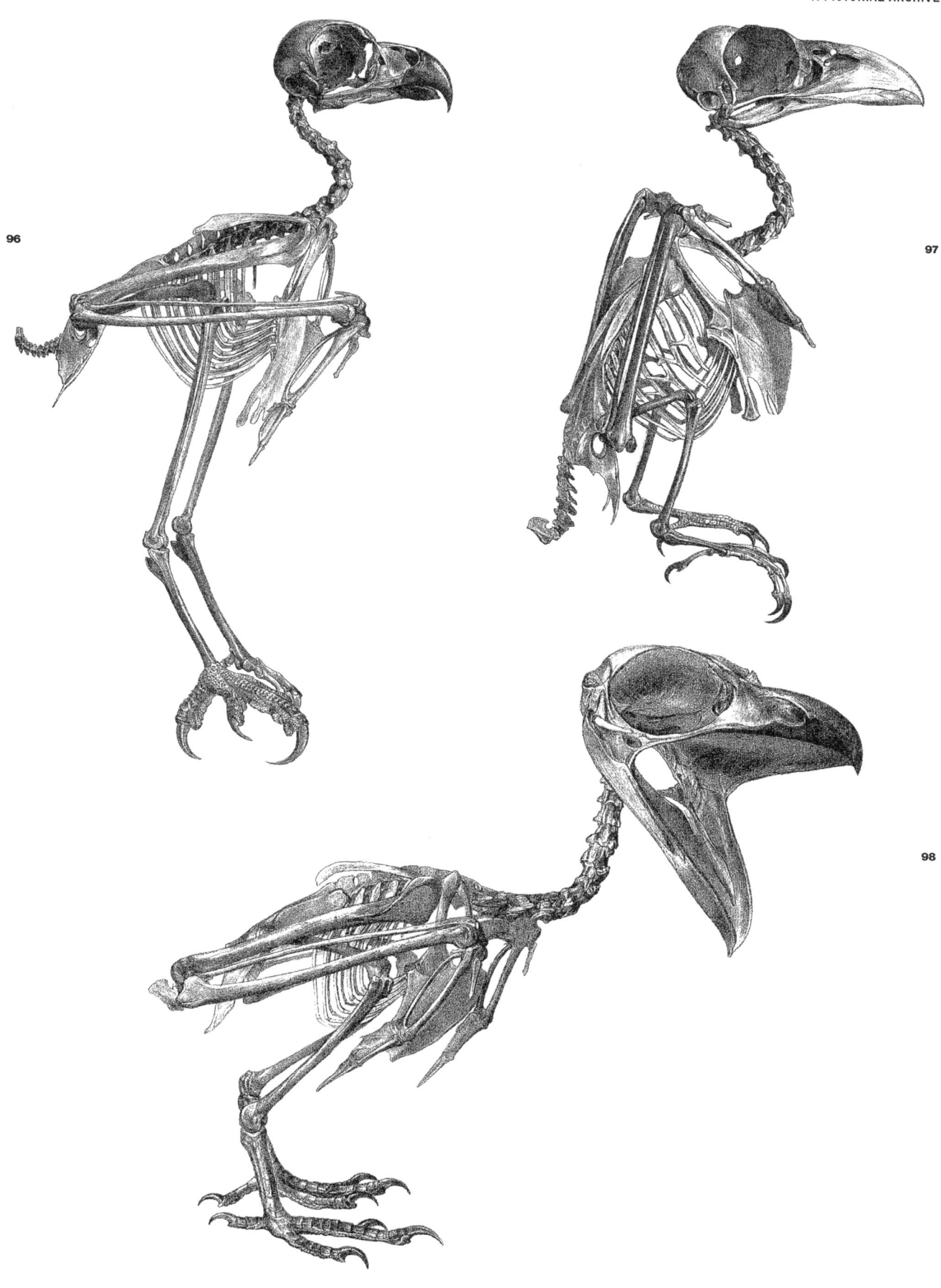

Fig.96 Ketupa Javanesis.

Fig.97 Eurystomus Orientalis.

Fig.98 Podargus Humeralis.

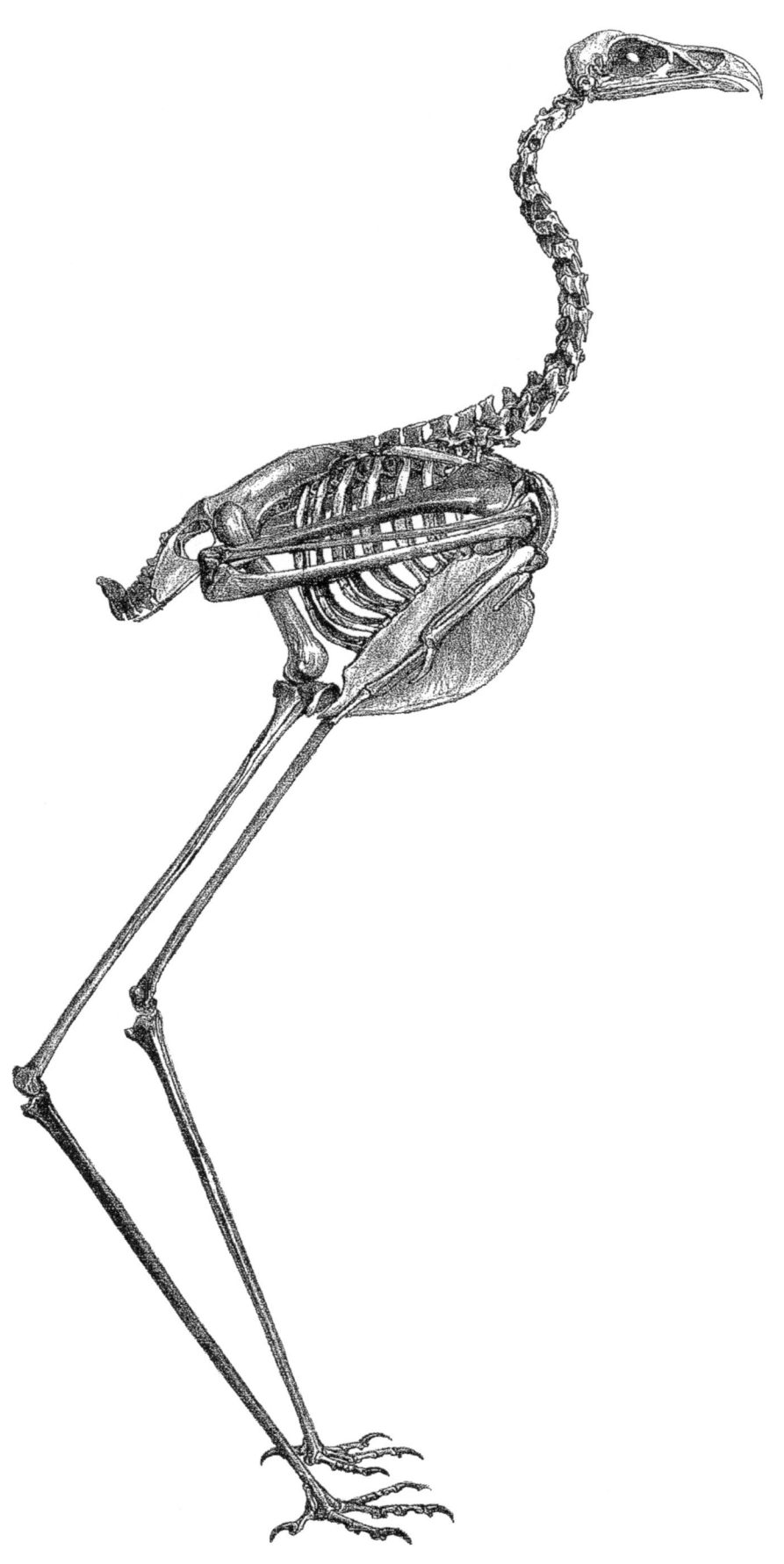

Fig.99 Serpentarius
Reptilivorus.

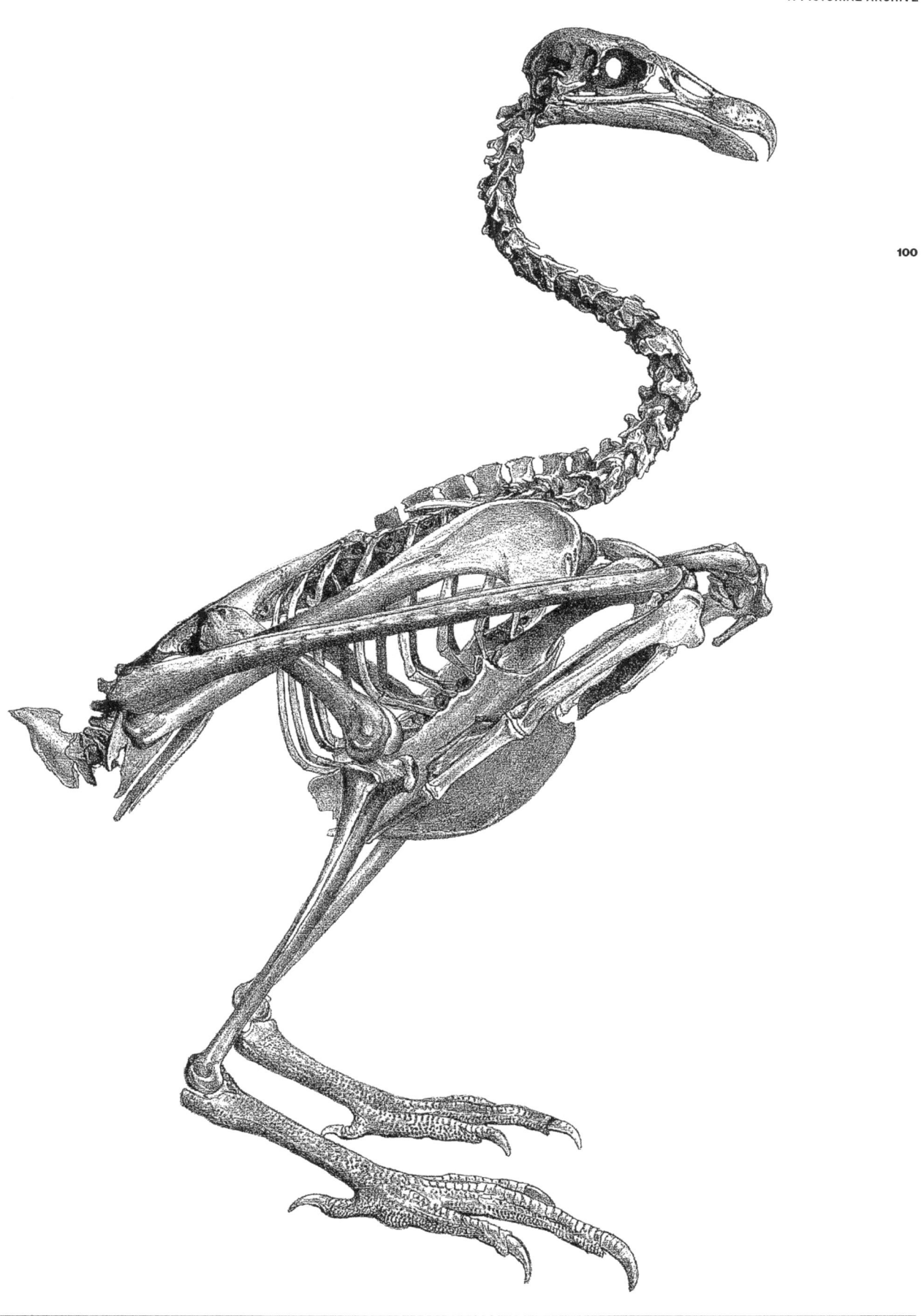

Fig.100 Sarcoramphus Gryphus.

Fig.101 Skeleton of unknown bird.

Fig.102 Skeleton of unknown bird.

Fig.103 Skeleton of unknown bird.

Fig.104 Skeleton of unknown bird.

Fig.104 Skeleton of a hen.

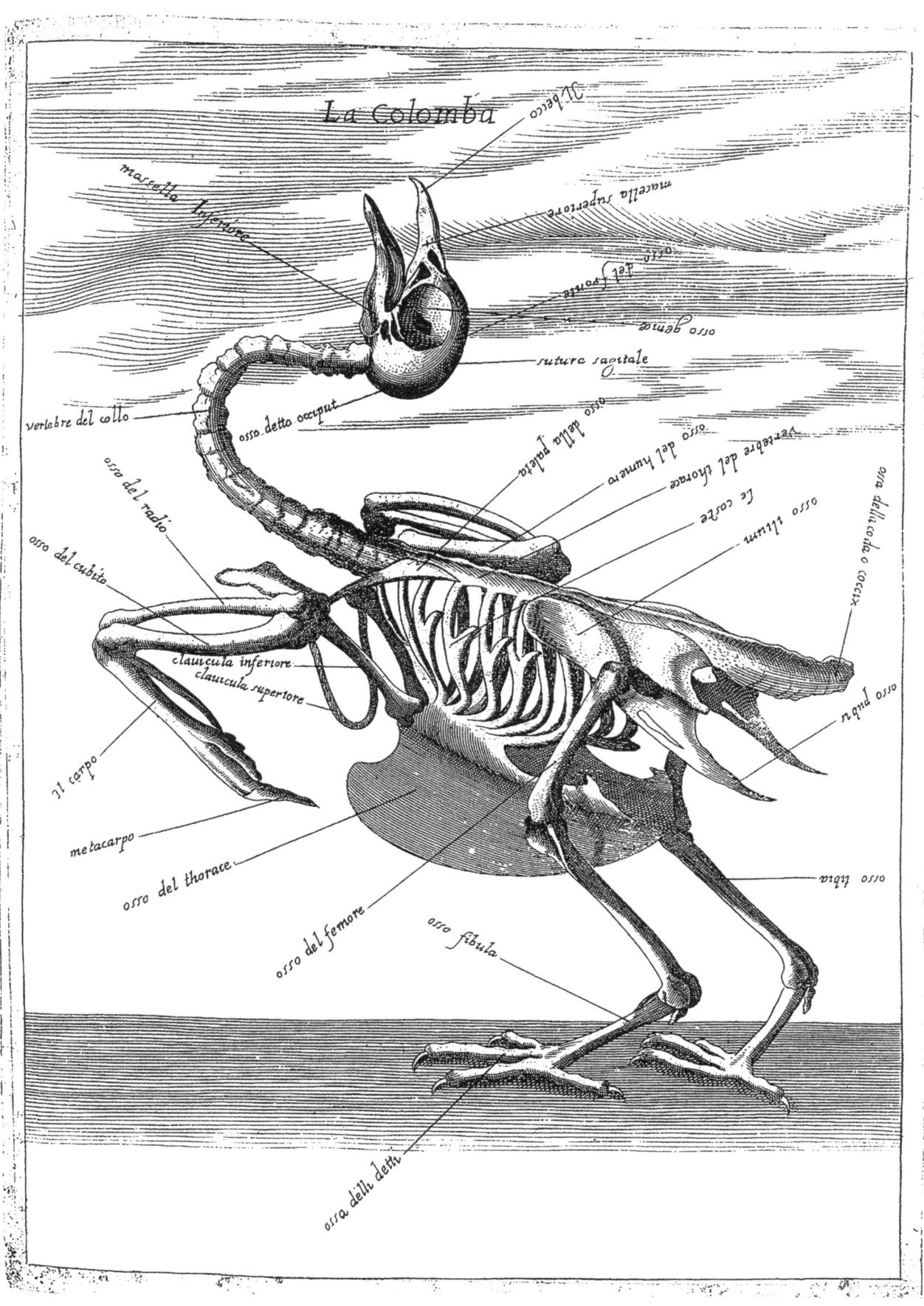

Fig.104 Skeleton of a dove.

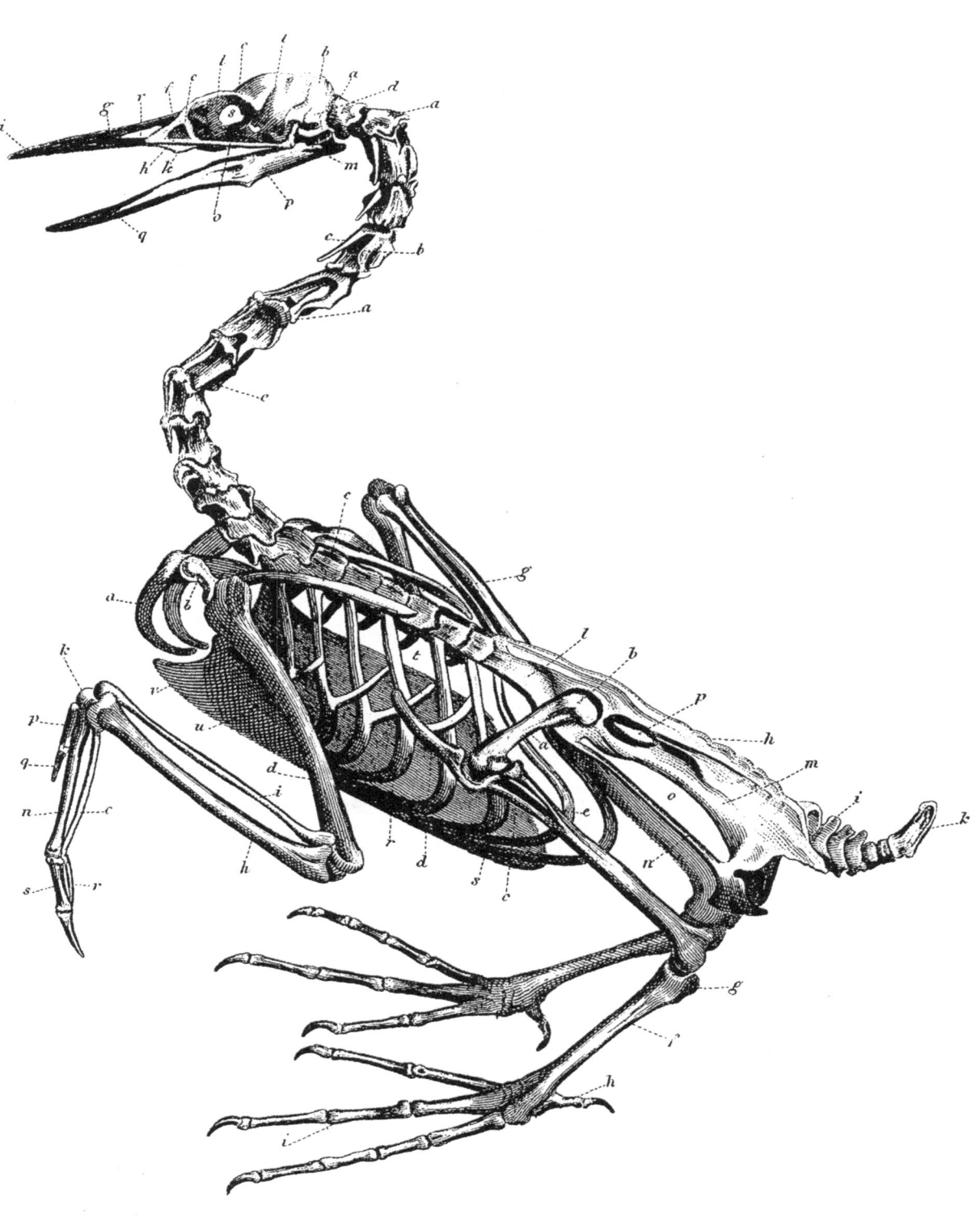

Fig.104 Skeleton of a hen.

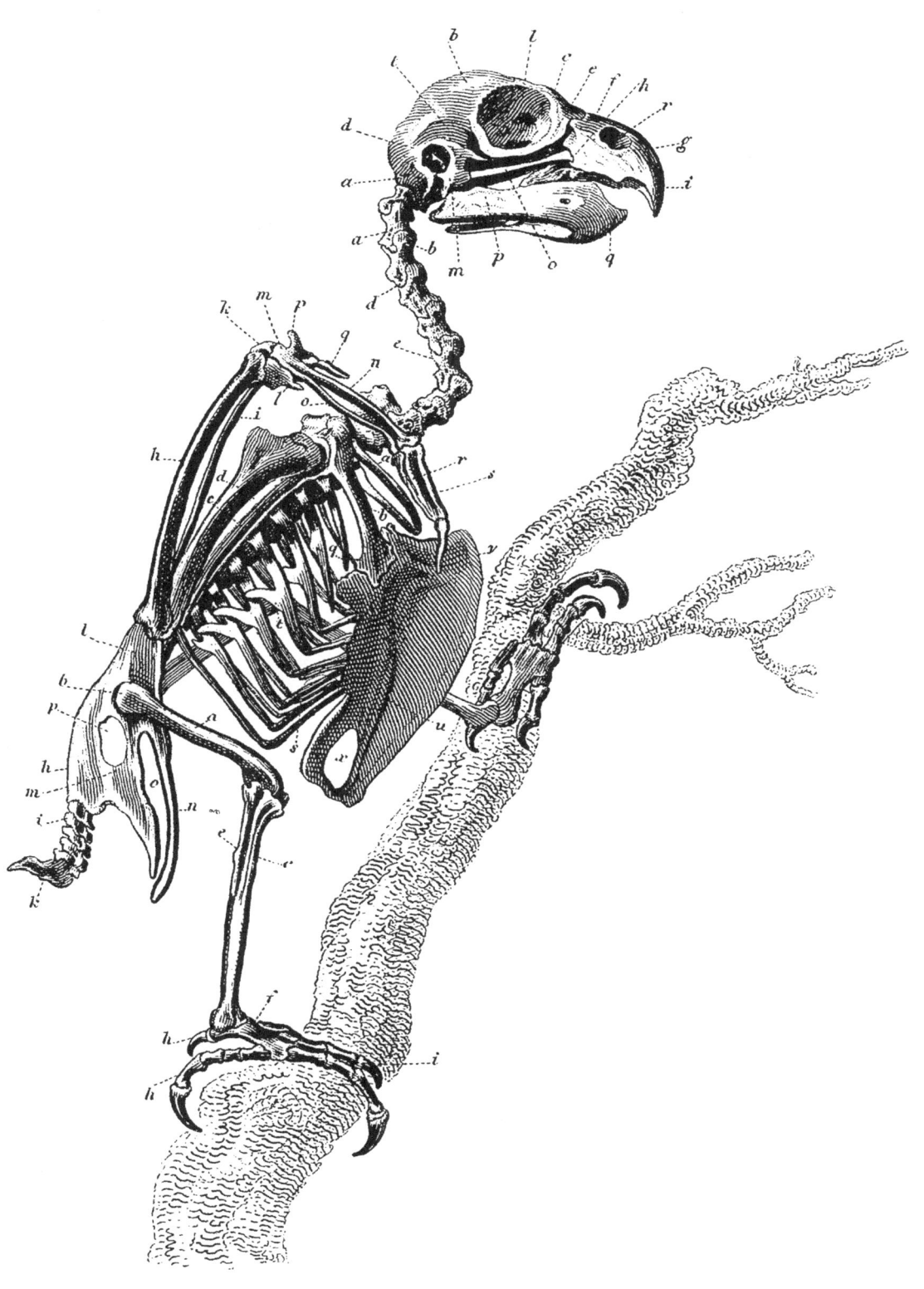

Fig.104 Skeleton of a hen.

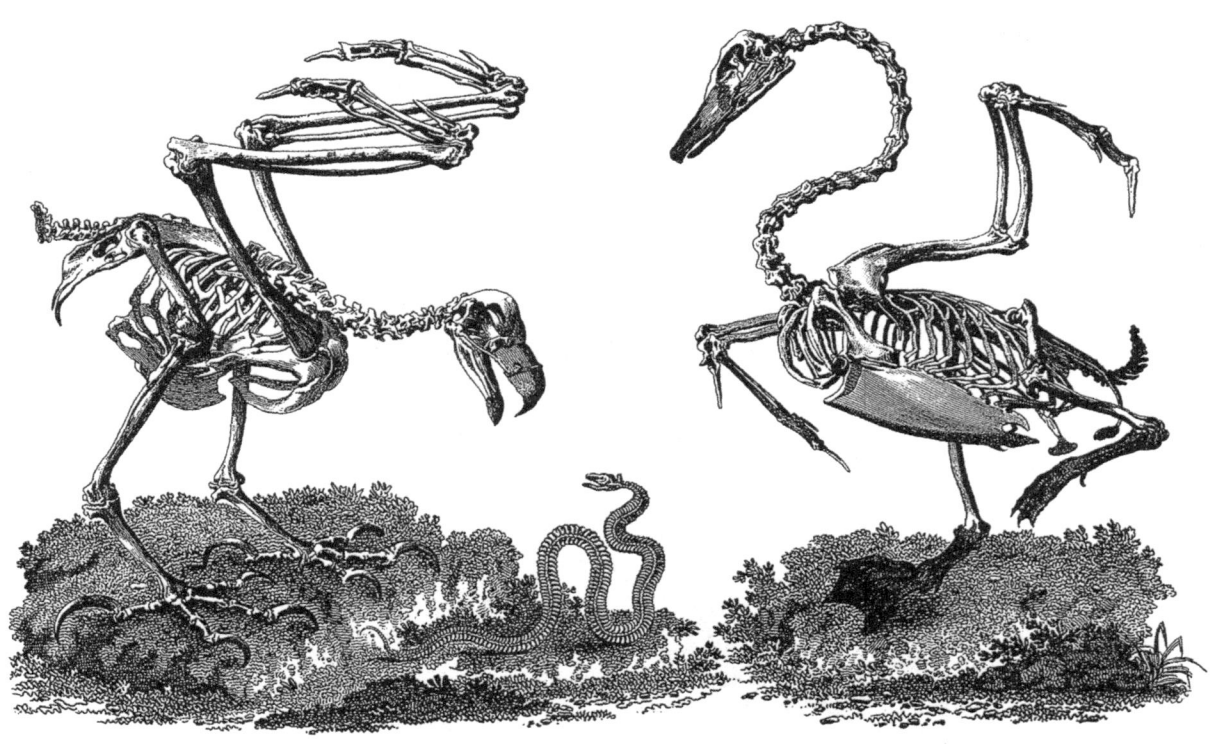

Eagle

Swan

Ostrich

Crane

Fig.104 Eagle, Swan, Ostrich & Crane.

Fig.104 Skeleton of a hen.

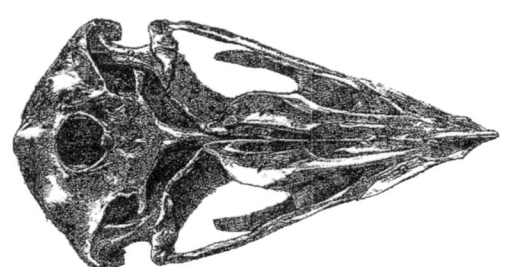
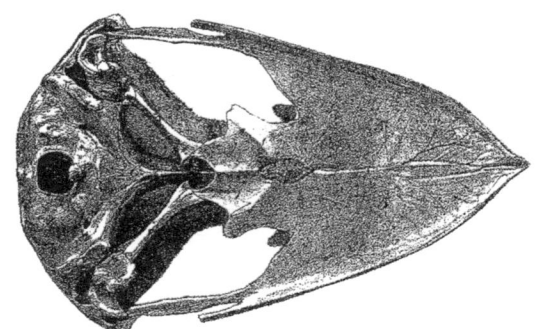
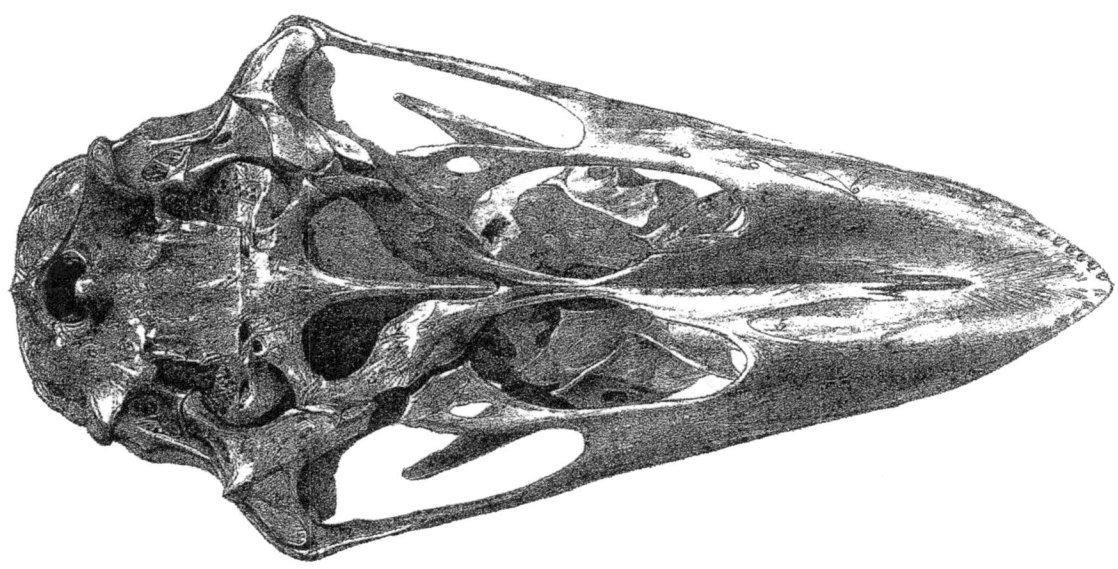

Fig.104 Skulls of unknow birds.

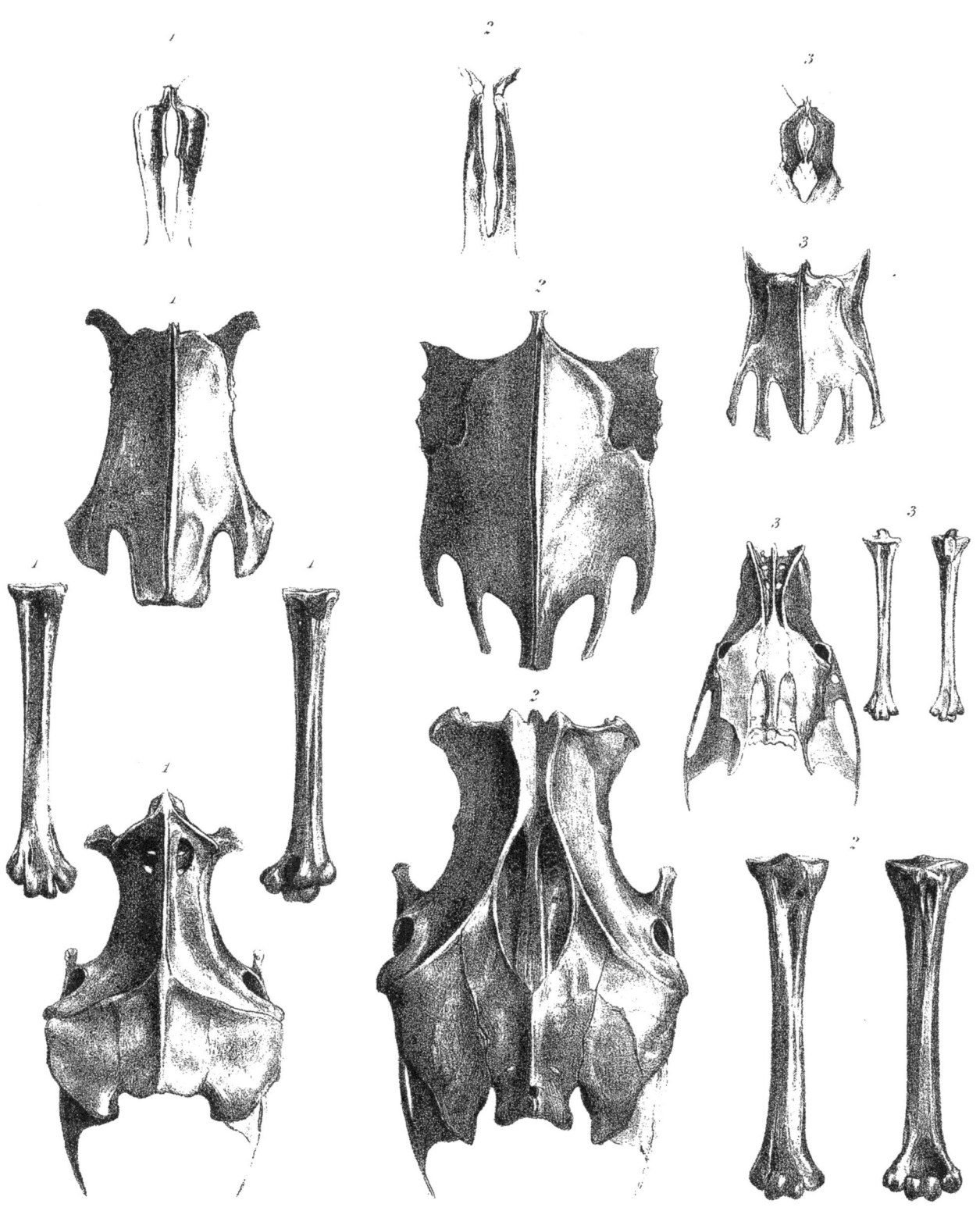

Fig.104 Skulls and bones of unknown birds.

Discover more at vaulteditions.com

Made in the USA
Coppell, TX
01 October 2020